A Passion for Wisdom

A Very Brief History of Philosophy

Robert C. Solomon and
Kathleen M. Higgins

Oxford University Press
New York / Oxford

Oxford University Press

Oxford   New York

Athens Auckland Bangkok Bogotá Buenos Aires Calcutta
Cape Town Chennai Dar es Salaam Delhi Florence Hong Kong Istanbul
Karachi Kuala Lumpur Madrid Melbourne Mexico City Mumbai
Nairobi Paris São Paulo Singapore Taipei Tokyo Toronto Warsaw

and associated companies in

Berlin   Ibadan

First published by Oxford University Press, Inc., 1997

First issued as an Oxford University Press paperback, 1998

Oxford is a registered trademark of Oxford University Press

Library of Congress Cataloging-in-Publication Data
Solomon, Robert C.
A passion for wisdom: a very brief history of philosophy / Robert C.
Solomon, Kathleen M. Higgins.
p.   cm.
Includes bibliographical references and index.
ISBN 0-19-511208-3 (alk. paper)
ISBN 0-19-511209-1 (pbk.)
1. Philosophy—History. I. Higgins, Kathleen Marie. II. Title.
B72.S655   1997   96-42034
109—dc20   CIP

1 3 5 7 9 10 8 6 4 2

Printed in the United States of America

for Jenene Allison
and Sarah Canright

Contents

Part III From Modernity to Postmodernism

Preface

The story of philosophy is the history of humanity's self-awareness and wonder with the world. It is, in short, collective and individual passion for wisdom. It encompasses, all at once, the origins of religion, mythology, cultural and personal self-identity, and science. It is a story that unfolds in philosophers' thoughts and teachings throughout the ages, but it can also be painted in broader brush strokes, giving us a larger picture of trends, movements, and grand sweeps of ideas—a picture of what nineteenth-century German philosophers called the *Zeitgeist*, the "spirit of the times," moving through time. Individual philosophers, of course, play major roles in the drama, but center stage belongs not to them but to the ideas they invented, discovered, or in any case promoted. The story is, accordingly, not so much a collective biography as it is an abstract portrait of the world of ideas.

What we have tried to present here is one version of that portrait. We have attempted to capture the global nature of philosophy as a (more or less) universal human attribute, but our perspective unavoidably is a Western one. Nevertheless, in Part I we have included a broad spread of traditions, from ancient America to Tibet, from Athens and Jerusalem to India, and the path from Plato to postmodernism. There is, of course, much more to be said, but too rarely is so much said so simply. The glory of philosophy, from our point of view, lies not so much in the details as in the expanse, and we invite the reader to marvel not so much at the depth as at the breadth of the history of human intelligence, passion, and imagination.

This book is a more concise version of our *Short History of Philosophy* (Oxford, 1996). We have omitted many of our editorial comments, and we are rather brief here on contemporary philosophy. As in our previous book, we have adopted a prudent policy of not discussing any living philosophers. We simply do not have the perspective to judge or even guess which of the current philosophical fads and fashions will still be of interest or influence in a decade or so, and we do not want to get into the business of declaring who now is important and who is not. But we do not want to give the impression that philosophy is a historical curiosity, a relic from the past. Philosophy is a dynamic, ongoing passion that is stepping out into all sorts of new directions, including a continuing reevaluation of its own history. We are delighted to have had the opportunity to be a small part of that never-ending process.

Timeline

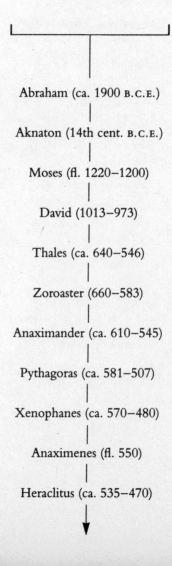

Abraham (ca. 1900 B.C.E.)

Aknaton (14th cent. B.C.E.)

Moses (fl. 1220–1200)

David (1013–973)

Thales (ca. 640–546)

Zoroaster (660–583)

Anaximander (ca. 610–545)

Pythagoras (ca. 581–507)

Xenophanes (ca. 570–480)

Anaximenes (fl. 550)

Heraclitus (ca. 535–470)

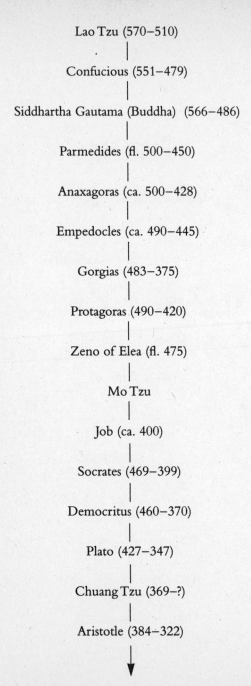

Lao Tzu (570–510)

Confucious (551–479)

Siddhartha Gautama (Buddha) (566–486)

Parmedides (fl. 500–450)

Anaxagoras (ca. 500–428)

Empedocles (ca. 490–445)

Gorgias (483–375)

Protagoras (490–420)

Zeno of Elea (fl. 475)

Mo Tzu

Job (ca. 400)

Socrates (469–399)

Democritus (460–370)

Plato (427–347)

Chuang Tzu (369–?)

Aristotle (384–322)

Theophrastus (ca. 372–287)

|

Mencius (372?–298?)

|

Pyrrho (360–270)

|

Epicurus (341–277)

|

Zeno the Stoic (336–265)

|

Diogenes (413–323)

|

Hsün Tzu (298–212)

|

Marcus Tullius Cicero (106–43 B.C.E.)

|

Lucretius (c. 94–c. 55)

|

Jesus Christ (ca. 5 B.C.E.–30 C.E.)

|

Philo (fl. 20 B.C.E.–4 C.E.)

|

St. Paul (ca. 10 C.E.–ca. 65 C.E.)

|

Epictetus (50–125)

|

Marcus Aurelius (121–180)

|

Nagarjuna (ca. 150–200)

|

Plotinus (ca. 205–269)

↓

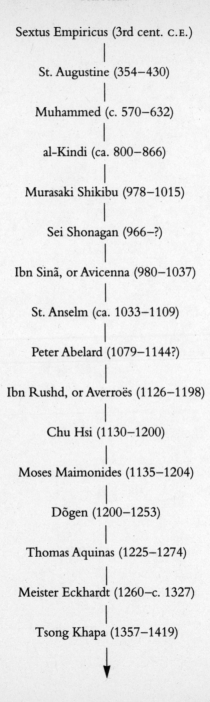

Sextus Empiricus (3rd cent. C.E.)

|

St. Augustine (354–430)

|

Muhammed (c. 570–632)

|

al-Kindi (ca. 800–866)

|

Murasaki Shikibu (978–1015)

|

Sei Shonagan (966–?)

|

Ibn Sinã, or Avicenna (980–1037)

|

St. Anselm (ca. 1033–1109)

|

Peter Abelard (1079–1144?)

|

Ibn Rushd, or Averroës (1126–1198)

|

Chu Hsi (1130–1200)

|

Moses Maimonides (1135–1204)

|

Dõgen (1200–1253)

|

Thomas Aquinas (1225–1274)

|

Meister Eckhardt (1260–c. 1327)

|

Tsong Khapa (1357–1419)

↓

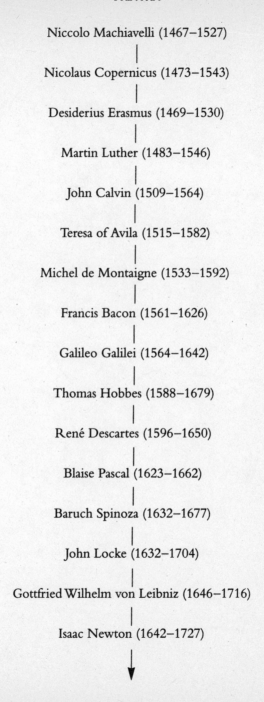

Niccolo Machiavelli (1467–1527)

Nicolaus Copernicus (1473–1543)

Desiderius Erasmus (1469–1530)

Martin Luther (1483–1546)

John Calvin (1509–1564)

Teresa of Avila (1515–1582)

Michel de Montaigne (1533–1592)

Francis Bacon (1561–1626)

Galileo Galilei (1564–1642)

Thomas Hobbes (1588–1679)

René Descartes (1596–1650)

Blaise Pascal (1623–1662)

Baruch Spinoza (1632–1677)

John Locke (1632–1704)

Gottfried Wilhelm von Leibniz (1646–1716)

Isaac Newton (1642–1727)

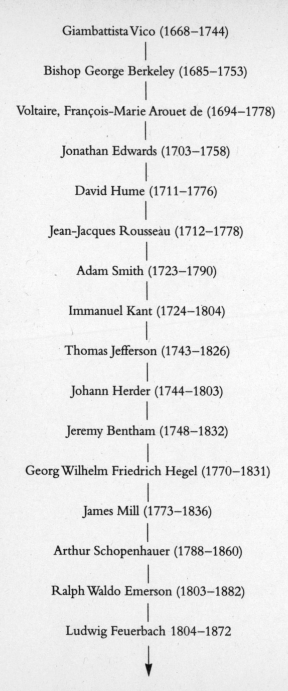

Giambattista Vico (1668–1744)

Bishop George Berkeley (1685–1753)

Voltaire, François-Marie Arouet de (1694–1778)

Jonathan Edwards (1703–1758)

David Hume (1711–1776)

Jean-Jacques Rousseau (1712–1778)

Adam Smith (1723–1790)

Immanuel Kant (1724–1804)

Thomas Jefferson (1743–1826)

Johann Herder (1744–1803)

Jeremy Bentham (1748–1832)

Georg Wilhelm Friedrich Hegel (1770–1831)

James Mill (1773–1836)

Arthur Schopenhauer (1788–1860)

Ralph Waldo Emerson (1803–1882)

Ludwig Feuerbach 1804–1872

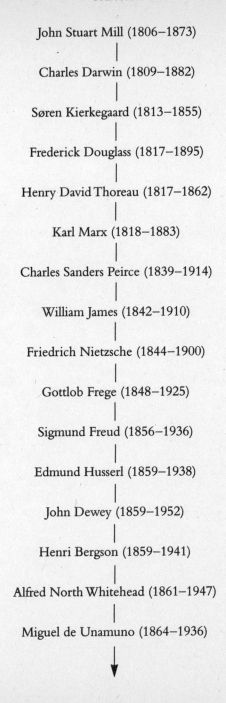

John Stuart Mill (1806–1873)

Charles Darwin (1809–1882)

Søren Kierkegaard (1813–1855)

Frederick Douglass (1817–1895)

Henry David Thoreau (1817–1862)

Karl Marx (1818–1883)

Charles Sanders Peirce (1839–1914)

William James (1842–1910)

Friedrich Nietzsche (1844–1900)

Gottlob Frege (1848–1925)

Sigmund Freud (1856–1936)

Edmund Husserl (1859–1938)

John Dewey (1859–1952)

Henri Bergson (1859–1941)

Alfred North Whitehead (1861–1947)

Miguel de Unamuno (1864–1936)

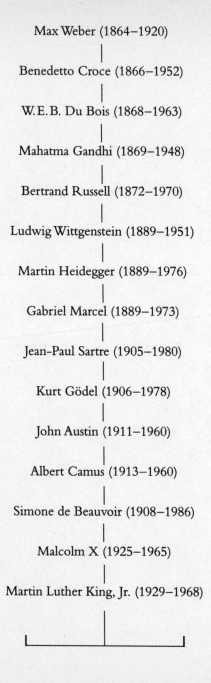

Max Weber (1864–1920)

Benedetto Croce (1866–1952)

W. E. B. Du Bois (1868–1963)

Mahatma Gandhi (1869–1948)

Bertrand Russell (1872–1970)

Ludwig Wittgenstein (1889–1951)

Martin Heidegger (1889–1976)

Gabriel Marcel (1889–1973)

Jean-Paul Sartre (1905–1980)

Kurt Gödel (1906–1978)

John Austin (1911–1960)

Albert Camus (1913–1960)

Simone de Beauvoir (1908–1986)

Malcolm X (1925–1965)

Martin Luther King, Jr. (1929–1968)

Part I

Is There Ultimate Truth?

In the Beginning

IF WE LOOK back at the whole of human existence, the appearance of philosophy and philosophers seems a curious phenomenon indeed, an ethereal secretion that cannot easily be explained in terms of physiology or physical necessity. Perhaps this notoriously "useless" activity was a byproduct of our oversized brains, the result of our thoughts overtaking our daily routines and looking beyond them. Philosophy was certainly one more complication of our expanding use of language, as a rich vocabulary of abstract and self-conscious concepts replaced our merely utilitarian and expressive grunts and growls. But philosophical ideas in some form—ideas about nature and its forces and questions about the soujourn of the soul in the afterlife, for instance—are virtually universal and can be traced back tens of thousands of years into prehistory. The Neanderthals had burial rituals and practices that suggest their belief in the continuing existence of the dead. Ideas about the existence of spirits, gods and goddesses, and active beings and forces beyond the bounds of direct human perception have a long history, too. Curiosity about nature, not just as a practical necessity but as genuine wonder, probably dates back to the Cro-Magnon. Various conceptions of collective self-identity and justice—not just the customs and habits of living together but the myths and rationalizations of territory, power, and community—no doubt antedate "civilization" by many centuries.

Somewhere between the sixth and fourth centuries B.C.E.,[1] however, fully articulated philosophical ideas and systems of thought began to appear in a number of far-flung places on the globe. Around the Mediterranean and the Middle East, in India and in China, philosophers appeared, great philosophers whose ideas would set the terms of philosophy in their various traditions for millennia to come. In the Middle East, the ancient Hebrews developed their conception of one God and of themselves as the "chosen people." In Greece, philosophers developed the first scientific theories of nature. In China, Taoists developed a very different vision of nature, while Confucius developed a powerful conception of society and the virtuous individual which rules Chinese thought even today. In ancient India, early Hindu theorists (the Vedantists) commented and speculated on the origin and nature of the world as described in the ancient Vedas and created a rich pantheon of gods, goddesses, and grand ideas.

PHILOSOPHY HAS NO single beginning, but it would be similarly naive to assume that philosophical thinking miraculously erupted spontaneously in various spots around the world. There were caravans across Asia and extensive trade around the Mediterranean, up and down the Nile, and throughout what we now call the Middle East. The early Hebrews were nomads, India was a crossroads for many different cultures, and Egypt was the source of ideas that later became the basis for Greek philosophy. There were great civilizations South of the Mediterranean as well, not only in Egypt but in Nubia (now Ethiopia) and further up the Nile. These cultures had sophisticated systems of astronomy, advanced mathematics, complex and thoughtful views of the nature of the soul, and an obsession with the question of life after death. Many of the leading ideas of Greek philosophy, including the all-important interests in geometry and the concept of the soul, were imported more or less directly from elsewhere. Indeed, it might be most accurate to see the great "miracle" of ancient Greece not as a remarkable beginning but as a culmination, the climax of a long story the beginnings of which we no longer remember.

[1] Since we will be talking about many philosophies and philosophers who were not Christians, we will use the accepted designation of "B.C.E"—or what is somewhat oddly designated "before the common era"—throughout this book. We will indicate uncertainty about dates with "ca."

PERHAPS THE OLDEST recorded philosophy comes from India. What we call Hinduism dates back thousands of years. Hinduism has not only a fabulous pantheon of gods and goddesses but a rich legacy of sages, speculation, and deep insights into the ways of the world. The ancient Hindu texts called the *Vedas* date back to 1400 B.C.E., and the *Upanishads*, which followed upon and commented on the *Vedas* (and are called *Vedanta*, or commentary) date from 800 B.C.E. Free-thinking arguments and a penchant for mysticism were already pervasive in Indian philosophy when the Buddha, Siddhartha Gautama (566–486 B.C.E.), appeared. (Jainism, a religion thoroughly committed to the sanctity of life and to nonviolence, appeared in India at about the same time.) For several centuries, Indian philosophers had defended a conception of absolute reality, or *Brahman*, which some insisted was utterly independent of and unknown to ordinary human experience. Following the Hindu scriptures in part, the Buddha developed a view according to which our ordinary picture of the universe and of ourselves is a kind of illusion. Both the early Vedantists and the Buddha argued that human suffering could only be transcended by seeing through the illusions of worldly reality and of the individual self. In his name, the Buddha's followers developed rich theories of knowledge, nature, the self and its passions, the human body and its ailments, the mind and its afflictions, and language and our ways of conceiving reality.

THE ANCIENT HEBREWS, of course, were another potent philosophical force in the ancient world. Their conceptions of a single God and of the God-given law set the stage for "Western civilization" a thousand years before Christ. (The Hebrew Decalogue—The Ten Commandments—was probably part of a larger canon of law already established by 1000 B.C.E.) There is perhaps no single Hebrew philosopher (before Jesus) who achieved the stature of Confucius, the Buddha, or Socrates. Nevertheless, the ancient Hebrew thinkers left us one of the most influential books in history—the Hebrew Bible, or "Old Testament." The book of Genesis in particular is one of the most important books in philosophy. Even though it is first of all a work of religion, it is also a history, sociology, and, some would say, science.

The ancient Hebrews did not invent the idea of the one God, nor were they the first ancient people to have an extensive body of law or to believe themselves "chosen." The fourteenth-century B.C.E. Egyptian Pharaoh Amenhotep IV (Aknaton) worshipped a single God; the

Babylonians under Hammurabi (1730–1685 B.C.E.) had an extensive legal code from which the Hebrews borrowed freely; and almost every tribe and society seems to have thought themselves special—as human societies still do. (Listen to virtually any national anthem.) The out-standing success of the ancient Hebrews lay in their skill at creating, reflecting upon and telling their own story—the story of a hearty people who made a contract with God, who suffered all kinds of catastrophes ultimately of their own making but who nevertheless endured.

ALSO IN THE Middle East, in what was known as Persia, a man named Zarathustra of Balkh, or Zoroaster (660–583 B.C.E.), began to move toward a comprehensive moral monotheism. We can speculate on the extent to which Zarathustra was influenced by the ancient Hebrews, the early Egyptian monotheist Ahknaton, and the Hindu Vedas (for whom his ideas show a remarkable affinity). One might deny that he really was a monotheist, for he did believe in a number of gods. Never-theless, he directed worship to the most powerful of the gods, the cre-ator god Ahura Mazda, and defended a powerful notion of good and evil as active forces in the world. According to Zarathustra, Ahura Mazda was on the side of the good, but both good and evil are present in all of us. He worried, a thousand years before the problem would be taken up in North Africa by Saint Augustine, about what has come to be called "the problem of evil": How can God allow so much suffering and wrongdoing in the world? In the hands of the later Manicheans (who were influenced by Zarathustra but considered heretics by the Zoroastrians), this moral dualism would become a cosmic battle between Good and Evil. The Zoroastrians would make Persia one of the most powerful empires in the world.

IN THE SIXTH century B.C.E., China was already a highly advanced political culture. But it was also a society in turmoil. Accordingly, Confucius (Kong Fuzi, 600–500 B.C.E.) developed a philosophy that was concerned almost entirely with social and political issues. He talked about harmonious relationships, leadership and statesmanship, getting along with and inspiring others, self-examination and self-transformation, and cultivating personal virtue and avoiding vice. The central aim of Confucianism was to define and cultivate the Way (*Tao*) to a harmonious society. It is no coincidence that Confuius should have adopted such an ambition during a period of political upheaval in

China, which is still viewed in Chinese history as the darkest of times. Unlike his contemporary the Buddha, Confucius had no intention of founding a religion, nor did he aim to overwhelm his countrymen with abstract philosophical brilliance or prophecy. After his death, however, he was admired and even deified by whole societies, and Confucianism—often along with Buddhism—is now the religion of one third of the world.

It was also in sixth century China that a second sage (or possibly a number of sages) called Lao Tzu developed a very different vision of the Way (*Tao*) to peace and enlightenment. (The Greek word *diké*, often translated as "justice," originally meant "the way" as well.) Unlike his contemporary Confucius, Lao Tzu attributed great importance to nature and correspondingly less to human society. Confucius thought certain passions "unnatural," for example, which essentially meant that they should play no part in the proper life of a gentleman. Lao Tzu, by contrast, had much more faith in nature and much more tolerance for the passions of uneducated, uncultivated men. For Confucius, the way to the good life is to follow the traditions of honor and respect set down by one's ancestors. For Lao Tzu, the Way is more mysterious. It cannot be spoken. It cannot be spelled out. It cannot be explained in a recipe or guidebook or a philosophy. According to Lao Tzu's *Tao Té Ching*, "The Tao that can be followed is not the true Tao; The name that can be named is not the true name." But that does not mean that one cannot find and try to live according to it, and Taoist teachings are intended to guide us on our way.

Between them, Confucius and Lao Tzu defined Chinese philosophy. They agreed on their overall emphasis on **harmony** as the ideal state of both society and the individual, and they insisted on an all-encompassing or "holistic" conception of human life that emphasizes a person's place in a larger context. For both Confucianism and Taoism, the development of personal character is the main goal in life, but the personal is not to be defined in individualistic terms. For the Confucian, the personal is the social. For the Taoist, the personal is the realtion to nature. Whatever their disagreements about the relative importance of nature and society, the Chinese thinkers were in considerable agreement on the necessity of harmony in human life and a larger sense of the "person" than the mere individual.

It is worth noting that China also had a technological tradition that goes back further than Western technology. The Chinese invented gunpowder, noodles, and eyeglasses, for example, centuries before the

West did. China has always taken a pragmatic, practical view of science as opposed to the quest for scientific knowledge for its own sake. Confucian philosophy, in particular, esteems scientific theory far less than social harmony. The remarkable history of technology in Asia has little to do with the much idealized "search for truth." For all of its emphasis on nature, Taoism has virtually nothing to do with science, and Buddhism sees not only science but the very idea of progress in the knowledge of nature as just another aspect of humanity's great illusion. These views are worth keeping in mind as we move, finally, to the philosophy of the ancient Greeks.

THE GREEKS (HELLENES) were a group of nomadic Indo-Europeans who came down from the north and replaced a people already settled by the Aegean Sea. They were not great innovators at first, but as they traded around the Mediterranean, the Greeks borrowed freely from other cultures. From the Phoenicians they borrowed an alphabet, some technology, and bold new religious ideas. From Egypt they borrowed the models that came to define Greek architecture, the basics of geometry, and some of the more exotic ideas of early Greek "mystery" religion. From Babylon (now Iraq) they borrowed astronomy, mathematics, geometry, and still more religious ideas. The Egyptian God Osiris became the Greek Dionysos, and in the sixth century, the powerful mystery cult of Dionysos spread across Greece teaching that human nature is part nature, part divine. This was taken to mean, among other things, that we have eternal life—not an unwelcome idea to a world in which life was often, in the famous phrase of the British philosopher Thomas Hobbes, "nasty, brutish and short."

Greek philosophy emerged from this mixture of mythology, mystery, and mathematics. The first Greek philosophers found themselves in both enviable and extremely vulnerable circumstances. Their culture was rich and creative, but they were surrounded by jealous and competitive enemies. It was not at all unusual for great cultures to be suddenly invaded and virtually wiped off the map of the known world, and what was not destroyed by war would often be devastated by nature. Epidemics swept through cities like silent armies. Life was unpredictable, often tragic, and therefore both precious and lamentable. "Better to never have been born," claimed the cheerful figure Silenus, "and next best to die soon."

In a world in which people had so little control, the concept of *fate* naturally played an important role. But whereas the Greeks at

Troy and then the Greeks of Homer's time attributed fate to the whimsical decisions of the gods and goddesses, the philosophers of the sixth century looked for an underlying order to things, some stable and comprehensible foundation. In place of the whims and passions of the gods and the uncertainties of fate, there had to be *logos*, some reason or underlying logic. Religion had opened the way to the "beyond" for thousands of years, but it was philosophy that would demand order in the beyond.

By the sixth century, the traditional mythology of Greece was already becoming a bit tired and increasingly problematic. The stories of the gods and goddesses and their various victims and escorts were no longer taken all that seriously, much less literally, by sophisticated Greeks. In the gap between the mundane and the fantastic, the idea of "the Truth" emerged. Suppose that we simply "made up" our gods and goddesses, complained Xenophanes (570–480 B.C.E.). "If oxen and horses and lions had hands and could draw as man does, horses would draw the gods shaped as horses and oxen like oxen, each making the bodies of the gods like their own." Why, Xenophanes asked, should we worship beings who have such notoriously bad manners, such flabby morals, and such childish emotions? Xenophanes thus recommended, at about the same time that the first books of the Hebrew Bible were being assembled, belief in "One god, greatest among gods and men, in no way like mortals in body or in mind."

We do not know how far these doubts extended through Greek society, but it is very clear that they were in the air. Monotheism was certainly known through the Hebrews, for there was considerable contact between the Hebrews and the Greeks. Monotheism must have also appealed to the Greek sense of unity, despite the plurality of Greek gods and goddesses. It was from such radical ideas that philosophy (from the Greek *philein*, love, and *sophia*, wisdom) was born in Greece.

Whence the World? Early Philosophy in India

The philosophy of ancient India is bound up with "Hinduism," but strictly speaking, there is no single set of philosophies—and for that matter no single religion—called "Hinduism." (*Hindu* is an Arabic word referring not to a religion but to a place, "east of the Indus river.") "Hinduism" refers rather indiscriminately to an enormous variety of beliefs, some of them theistic, some of them not; some of

them mystical, others not; some of them steeped in ancient Indian
mythology, others not. It also refers to a particular social system, the
caste system, which was rationalized by Hindu philosophy.

Traditional Hinduism is populated with fantastic creatures and
divinities at least as imaginative as anything in Greek mythology.
There is central trinity of gods, Brahma (the creator god), Vishnu
(the god who maintains the universe), and Shiva (the god of destruction). But these are the faces of one God, of one reality rather than
many. (This view is sometimes called "henotheism.") The familiar
depictions of Shiva point to a bewildering religious complexity in
which the gods routinely take on various forms and manifestations,
adopt different personae, serve very different functions, and, accordingly, have many different names. Shiva's consort, Parvati, for example, is represented in some myths by the very sensual Uma and in
others by the maternal Amba, the destructive Kali, or Shakti, Shiva's
source of power.

The central importance of goddesses in Hinduism is particularly
worth noting given the overwhelming male bias of most of the
world's other major religions. Also evident and appealing in Hindu
mythology are its imaginative playfulness and its relative lack of inhi-
bition and dogmatism, at least in the many different concepts of the
divine. In even the most playful Hindu tales, however, we find the
enduring themes of renewal, the continuity of life, and the Oneness
of the Universe, however many its manifestations or appearances.

AS A PHILOSOPHY, however, Hinduism is best identified by that set
of writings known as the *Vedas*. The earliest Vedas, the *Rg Veda*, may
have been written nearly 1500 years B.C.E., hundreds of years before
Moses and six hundred years before Homer. The Vedas are a combination of poetry, hymns, mythology and cosmogony—the "personal"
origins of the universe. Later commentaries on the Vedas, the *Upanishads* or *Vedanta*, further focus the story of creation on *Brahman*—
absolute reality (as distinguished from Brahma, the king of the gods).
The theory of Brahman, like the rich mythology of earlier India, was
shot through with ambiguity and contradiction, not by way of per-
versity but in order to make a single point (one that would be akin to
the earliest philosophy of the Greeks): that there is one substance
(Brahman) underlying infinitely many manifestations.

The idea that there are many gods, all of whom are manifestations of
the same God, is no doubt bewildering to monotheists and polytheists

alike, if they think of godliness as an inherently stable quality. Indian philosophy will also seem bewildering or incoherent to those who insist on not only the singularity but the ultimate rationality of reality, and on its unchanging existence. Brahman is unchanging only in the sense that it is always changing.

The Vedas begin with cosmogony, the question of origins: Why is there anything? It is worth noting that even the earliest Vedas display considerable skepticism as to whether such ultimate questions are answerable at all. "Whence this creation has arisen— perhaps it formed itself, or perhaps it did not— the one who looks down on it, in the highest heaven, only he knows— or perhaps he does not know." The early Vedas also raise the question of what the universe was like before the creation. Is the world is itself an illusion? Perhaps it is "not even nothing." It is in India that we first hear the familiar stories of an original progenitor who creates the world and all things in it. The sexual imagery in these stories is candid, and it would not be inaccurate to see early Indian cosmogony, like most of the cosmogonies of the ancient world, as personifications of the cosmos, as an attempt to understand creation through the more immediate understanding of human procreation. Indeed, the *Rg Veda* casts the universe itself as a cosmic immortal person.

This basic concern with the person pervades Indian philosophy, and it is evident in the perpetual concern for the self, the soul, and the true nature of the individual person. The same concerns would preoccupy Buddhism and Jainism, which emerged from Hinduism hundreds of years later. On the one hand, there is the conception of the individual soul, or *jiva*, which distinguishes each individual as a unique being. Whether or not this *jiva* is genuine or is in any way substantial enough to survive the death of the body is a matter of fascinating debate. On the other hand, the self is referred to as *atman*, which might be understood as the principle of life that exists in every human being. Thus we might see each individual as a *jiva* vitalized by an *atman*, or, quite differently, we might come to see *jiva* as a false self and *atman* as the true self. The Vedas make clear that we are not to think of *jiva* and *atman* as two selves fighting for superiority within a person. The true nature of the self has been one of the focal points of philosophy in India for three thousand years.

Can we know Brahman, ultimate reality? If so, how? Here we can locate what is best known (in the West) about Indian philosophy — its *mysticism* and that familiar set of exercises known as *yoga*. It would be an enormous mistake to think of Indian philosophy, even in its most ancient forms, as *nothing but* mysticism, the favorite excuse of many Western philosophers for ignoring Indian philosophy altogether. But the skeptical doubts of the oldest Vedas continue to haunt the idea that Brahman can be comprehended through reason or reflection alone. Knowledge of Brahman may come through an all-embracing, unifying mystical experience.

In Indian philosophy, one is not simply surprised by such an experience, as some unprepared Christians, notably Paul on his way to Damascus, have claimed to have experienced visions of Christ or the Virgin Mary or the Holy Grail. One needs ample preparation, which includes, among other things, a thorough study and understanding of the Vedas and Upanishads and certain ritual practices such as meditation and yoga. To have the experience of Brahma, *brahmavidya*, one must be "fit." This fitness does not refer primarily to health or body tone (although such matters are not ignored), nor is relaxation as such a proper aim of yoga. Yoga is self-discipline, the spiritual self-discipline that will allow a person to reach a deeper reality and have a blissful experience in doing so.

This blissful experience lies at the heart of almost all Indian philosophy, although it goes by various names and is approached by very different doctrines and techniques. Buddhists refer to it as *Nirvana*, Jains as "liberation from suffering," and Vedantins as *mukti*, but they interpret its nature and its significance very differently. Some would say that what we call reality is an illusion, and that the mystical experience of Brahman allows us to perceive the truly real for the first time. Others would allow that our everyday world is real enough, but that it is a superficial reality, one with many levels and depths; and that at bottom, reality is Brahman, the One. In all three traditions— Hinduism, Buddhism, and Jainism—the ultimate aim is to achieve a certain freedom from the troubles and concerns of everyday existence. On a more metaphysical level, such "liberation from suffering" results in freedom from the recurrent cycle of death and rebirth, in which all beings are bound.

The Hebrew People, Their God, and the Law

Tracing itself back to the third millennium B.C.E. to the patriarch Abraham, Judaism has been a rich source of philosophy and philosophical disputation—first in the self-conception of the Hebrew people and their law, later in the teachings of the prophets (ninth to eighth century B.C.E.), and finally in the extensive writings that became the Talmud, the body of law and commentaries based on the Torah. (The word "Jewish" comes from the name of the Kingdom of Judah, which after the death of Solomon comprised two of the twelve tribes of Israel.) Philosophical argument became so basic to the life of the ancient Hebrews that there was no need to distinguish it as a separate intellectual enterprise. Because of their commitment to the law, the Hebrews were perpetually interested in questions about the meaning of the law and how it instructed people to live, in questions about justice and the good society. Above all, the Hebrews were vitally interested in how they were to please their all-powerful, not always predictable God. Hebrew philosophy, accordingly, was primarily concerned with the nature of this God and the significance of the laws he had given to his people. The law would become central to Hebrew and later Jewish religious thinking in a way that it had not to any other people.

Ancient Hebrew philosophy was largely defined by these three key concepts: the belief in a single God, the sense of being favored or "chosen" by that God, and the importance of the God-given law. The second, perhaps, might be dismissed as overly chauvinistic and too ethnically exclusive for philosophy, but the first and third concepts not only define the philosophy of the ancient Hebrews but provide the framework for virtually the entire course of Western history and philosophy, the One God and His Law.[2]

Philosophically, the idea of a single, all-powerful God implied universality, a single set of rules and beliefs that would apply not only in this or that region or city-state but everywhere and to everyone. It is not entirely clear when the ancient Hebrews adopted their belief in one God, but it clearly followed a period during which they, too, acknowledged a plurality of competing gods and goddesses, one of whom became their favorite and who, in return, made them his "chosen people."

This compromise between monotheism and polytheism anticipated

[2]   We are very aware of and sensitive to the issues surrounding the masculine "He" in the designation of God, and it may well be true that many of the religions preceding Judaism, Christianity, and Islam, and against which they rebelled, were matriarchal in form. But insofar as we are talking about those religions in their traditional conceptions, we will employ the masculine pronoun.

a number of complex problems that would prompt a good deal of Jewish, Christian, and Islamic theology. One enduring philosophical problem had to do with the relationship of the one God to Creation. Did God create a world that was independent of himself, or is He present in the world? How and why did He create the universe, and why did he do it as he did it? Why, in particular, did he create people "in his image," as the English translation of the Hebrew Bible puts it, and what is his continuing relationship with them?

The opening book of the Hebrew Bible, the book of Genesis, presents God as the all-powerful Creator who created the different orders of beings in steps, on six consecutive "days," culminating in the creation of human beings. Jewish scripture departed from the common Middle Eastern tendency to see the world as subsequent to previous worlds and conditions. In India, the world may have not been eternal, but it was unimaginably old (three trillion years or so). Even for the Greeks, the idea that the world could come into being *from nothing* was all but incomprehensible. By contrast, Judaism holds that God created the world out of nothing. Needless to say, there has been a great deal of disputation about the proper interpretation of Genesis, beginning long before Charles Darwin added a radically new wrinkle with the idea that life was originally created according to a process rather than all at once. But what has been most discussed and debated in and since the Hebrew Bible is God's relationship to one of his creations, human beings. If man was created "in God's own image," why would God favor some people over others, as the Hebrews believed he had favored them? But the effect of this belief on the Hebrews was astounding. A ragtaggle of nomads emerged from their "exodus" a determined and enduring nation. It was the most powerful of ancient ideas.

Although Judaism emphasizes the dignity of the individual, we must remember that it began as a tribal religion. The individual has meaning and dignity insofar as he or she is a member of the community; but as in so many ancient societies, the formation of community is not left to chance. Judaism considers its status as "the Chosen People" to mean chosen by virtue of God's promise to their ancestor Abraham. Abraham was promised by God that his descendants would become a great nation. There is, accordingly, an exclusive, even racial element to Judaism, which would be firmly rejected by the early Christians, especially by Saint Paul. According to this ancient viewpoint, Jewishness is not so much a philosophy or a set of beliefs, as it is a matter of membership. Consequently, Jewish philosophy is not nearly as focused on the intricacies of theology and belief as on the meaning of membership in the Jewish community and the implications of that membership.

THERE IS LITTLE by way of theology in the Hebrew Bible, but the personality of God, if we may call it that, is rendered as clearly as if in a novel. The God of the Hebrews is, by his own admission, a jealous God. He is sometimes an angry God, a wrathful God. Any number of familiar stories from the Hebrew Bible or Old Testament could be used to illustrate the point, but the philosophical thesis—which one might compare with the early Greek view of Fate—is that the Hebrews' all-powerful, protecting God was highly unpredictable and tempestuous, even whimsical. He could be easily enraged, as the disasters that befell the Hebrews proved. On the one hand, the Hebrews were protected by their mighty God. On the other hand, this protection was by no means wholly reliable, and the lapses in God's protection had to be explained. The same problem arose concerning God's *grace*. In Judaism as in much of Christianity, grace was bestowed by God as a matter of pure choice on His part. No one and no people was entitled to it.

The philosophy of the Hebrews must be understood in terms of this great anxiety regarding the Hebrew *covenant* with God. The covenant gave them some assurance, so that when disaster struck—as it so often did, the Jews did not doubt their belief in God but rather *blamed themselves*. The prophets would speak almost with pride of the forces amassed against Israel, not as proof of God's abandonment but rather as proof of his displeasure with the Jewish people. The alternative interpretation—that they were being abandoned by God—was unthinkable to the Hebrews. Guilt was far preferable to the loss of faith; it might be said that the Hebrews gave guilt its philosophical form. But in so doing, they also pushed human self-examination to depths it had never known before.

Why Suffering? Zoroastrianism and the Problem of Evil

The notion of a single God seems to have come from a number of sources, including not only Aknaton in ancient Egypt and the Hebrews but in Persia and the philosophy of Zoroastrianism. Philosophically,

Zoroastrianism is of special interest for its original confrontation with the philosophical problems associated with the conception of a single Creator God. Hebrew philosophy emphasized obedience to God and his law, but Zoroastrianism was perhaps the first philosophy to focus on the objective nature of good and evil.

Zarathustra opposed the polytheistic practices of his contemporaries and devoted himself to the worship of Ahura Mazda, whom he credited with the creation of the world. But Zarathustra acknowledged the reality of lesser deities, who were created by Ahura Mazda and who existed in union with him. These lesser deities were associated with particular aspects of nature, which worshippers addressed directly in the process of worshipping these divinities. This worship of nature was, of course, one of the oldest forms of religion, and nature worship was evident at about the same time in Greek and other Middle Eastern traditions, often coexisting with anthropomorphic and abstractly spiritual religions. The same was true of Zoroastrianism. Although devoted to Ahura Mazda as the supreme God, Zoroastrians considered worship of fire (and the sun, as a creature of fire) to be a duty; they believed the soul would be purified by fire. Zoroastrians were sometimes called "fireworshippers" as a result.

It is mainly from Zoroastrianism that we inherit *the problem of evil*, the question of how needless suffering, pain, and death can exist if in fact a good and powerful God created and watches over the world. If God were not good, if he were not in any sense a loving or a caring god, then the prevalence of suffering and the inevitability of death would not present a theological problem. Indeed, mutilation and death at the hands of the Greek Olympian gods and goddesses were accepted as a matter of course (although one could ask, in any particular case, why the god or goddess in question had suddenly turned on the victim). The Hindu god Shiva was explicitly designated the god of destruction. When he destroyed, there was no philosophical paradox, no theological problem to be solved; Shiva was just being Shiva. Similarly, when the evil goddess Kave of the Nukuoro Atoll (in the South Pacific) caused destruction, no further explanation was necessary.

In the history of the Hebrews, however, questions about God's reasons were unavoidable. When the Hebrew God allowed his "chosen" people to be sold into slavery and allowed Jerusalem and the Temple to be destroyed (not once but several times), the Hebrews faced a profound and deeply disturbing choice. They could either conclude that their God had broken his covenant and abandoned them, or they could conclude that they themselves had broken the covenant and betrayed God's trust. The question was unavoidable: Why would he do this? Even Jesus asked, "Why have you forsaken me?" The same question would repeat itself, thousands of years later, after the *Shoah* or Nazi Holocaust, in mid-twentieth-century Germany. The philosophy of the Hebrews (and much of Western thought more generally) is built upon this emphasis on blame and responsibility. The Genesis account of the first sin, "the Fall," suggested that evil came into the world through human choice.

This correspondence between responsibility and consequence could be called into question. In Jewish literature itself, the connection between sin and disaster was challenged in a most dramatic way. The Book of Job (possibly written during the Babylonian exile, around 400 B.C.E.) tells the story of a good man who is horribly punished despite his faithful obedience of all of God's laws. Satan taunts God by suggesting that Job behaves righteously only because God treats him well. God "tests" Job by allowing Satan to cause the worst personal disasters to befall Job and his family. Through it all, Job continues to live as piously as he always has, although he frequently implores God to help him. In the end, God restores Job to his former happy state, but he also insists that his ways need not be comprehensible to human beings. Thus the need for faith despite the apparent injustice in the world. But this conclusion leaves the problem of evil horribly unresolved. Why should a just man suffer for no reason? The Book of Job illustrates the terrifying and unpredictable relationship that the Jews felt they had with their God.

Another way around the problem of evil is the introduction of a second powerful being, Satan or the Devil. Zarathustra explained suffering as the consequence of a war between two twin spirits, the first spirits that Ahura Mazda created. One of these spirits is good; the other is destructive. The entire world is a manifestation of a battle between these two, between good and evil. This is in the Book of Job, for example, so it can be argued that Satan, not God, inflicted on Job his unjust punishments. But if this malevolent being were strong enough to counter the will of God, the God of the three great Western religions would not be all-powerful and he would not be the one God, either. Even if Satan is not strong enough to counter the will of God, his existence brings us back to our original question: How could a loving God allow evil to take place? After all, Satan is also one of God's creatures, and the destructive spirit was created by Ahura

Mazda. Moreover, what is our personal responsibility in the face of these overwhelming cosmic powers?

According to Zarathustra, the problem of evil is answered not only by postulating warring moral forces but also by insisting that human beings have a free moral choice. They can ally themselves with one or the other spirit, the good or the bad. As a religion, Zoroastrianism engages the believer and encourages commitment to the good spirit in all thoughts, words, and deeds. Moreover, Zarathustra promises this alliance will prove to be rewarding: at the end of this world, Zarathustra will lead those allied with the good spirit to an eternally blessed existence. This attractive thesis would find its (super)natural home in the philosophy of Christianity.

What Is Enlightenment? Buddhism and Jainism

In ancient India, the Buddha appeared in the sixth century B.C.E., and the religion called Jainism dates back at least that far. Both Buddhism and Jainism had formulated deep and intriguing accounts of the soul and human (and, in Jainism, the nonhuman) nature. Buddhism, in particular, tends to reject both the notion of Brahman and the notion of self (*atman*) that are so central to much of Hindu thought. Socially, both the Buddhists and the Jains rejected the Hindu caste system.

Nevertheless, Hinduism, Jainism, and Buddhism share a great many similarities, including respect for the Vedas. Despite a long history of mutual as well as internal disputation and argument, the Hindus, Jains, and Buddhists have not, for the most part, been particularly proselytizing or competitive. This is not to deny, of course, that sectarian groups in India (as in most parts of the world) have found frequent occasions for mutual slaughter. But until the arrival of the Europeans and Islam, the many myths and philosophies of Hinduism coexisted and often mixed and blended with Buddhism and Jainism and other local religions.

Perhaps most striking to the Western reader is the powerful combination of mysticism and logic in India, two fields of philosophy (insofar as either is considered to be "in" philosophy) that are usually envisioned as far apart or, indeed, flatly opposed to one another. But in India, mysticism in one form or another, the notion of a trance-like blissful experience, would become the focal point of all three major religions. (The Sanskrit word for "philosophy" means "seeing.") All three traditions would also develop powerful logics, both in support of mystical experience and as weapons against those who would compromise the integrity of such experiences. Mysticism could be compromised through over-intellectualization, excessive attachment to the things of the everyday world, or uncritical dependence on the categories of common sense.

Both Buddhism and Jainism pay special attention to the nature of suffering and liberation from suffering. Jains take as their primary principle "Do no harm," and they practice respect for life—all life—even to the point of taking care that they do not crush the insects on the ground beneath them or accidentally inhale those flying in the air. The Buddha was deeply concerned about the horrible suffering he saw around him, and he denounced the caste system because it increased human suffering. The Buddha's basic philosophy, however, is concerned primarily with the individual's *inner* transformation, achieved by means of insight into the "Four Noble Truths" of Buddhism:

1. Life is suffering.
2. Suffering arises from selfish craving.
3. Selfish craving can be eliminated.
4. One can eliminate selfish craving by following the right way.

This right way to liberation or enlightenment is called the *Eightfold Path* of Buddhism, which consists of (1) right seeing, (2) right thinking, (3) right speech, (4) right action, (5) right effort, (6) right living, (7) right mindfulness, and (8) right meditation. The aim of Buddhism is to free oneself from deluded belief in the ego and all that goes with it—desire and frustration, ambition and disappointment, pride and humiliation—and to gain enlightenment and the end of misery, a condition called *Nirvana.* Nirvana is typically described in terms of the negation of the egoistic perspective and the cessation of suffering, but it can be positively understood as bliss, although it would be misleading to characterize the aim of Buddhism in terms of the Western ideal of "happiness."

Buddhists believe that all of life is impermanent. Reality amounts to a series of momentary existences; there are no enduring substances. A similar delusion leads us to believe that our egos have reality. In fact, there is no permanent self or soul. A human being is just a temporary composite of body, feeling, thoughts, dispositions, and consciousness. There is no larger eternal self (what the Vedantins call atman). There is only *anatman,* "no atman," no self. Recognition of the impermanence of both self and all objects of desire is a step toward insight and the end of misery. (Jains, by contrast, hold onto the belief in an individual self or soul, not only in human beings but in every living thing. This is why their respect for all life is so uncompromising—they believe, like many Hindus, that human souls may be reborn in animals.)

Although nothing persists, the Buddhists believe that every "condition" of the world arises from another, and that reality involves an extensive, ultimately all-inclusive causal chain, linking everyone and everything to all else, before and after. Rebirth and *karma* are aspects of this complex causal network. One might think of karma as the residue of the actions and activities a person performs over his or her lifetime and the key to a person's status in rebirth and reincarnation.

BUDDHISM DEVELOPED MANY schools of thought. Early on, there was a serious separation of Southern Buddhists (mainly in and near India), who focussed their attention on personal enlightenment, and Northern (Mahayana) Buddhists (in Tibet, Nepal, China, Japan, and Korea), who insisted on the primacy of compassion and regard for the less fortunate. The Southern Buddhists taught that enlightenment is to be found in an extremely ascetic and isolated monastic life, and that enlightenment is thus limited to a few. The Northern Buddhists, by contrast, insisted that everyone must be freed from suffering and spiritual ignorance, so those who are already enlightened must "stay back" to help those who live more or less ordinary lives. Such a person is a *Bodhisattva*. Bodhisattvas do not enter the state of Nirvana when they reach enlightenment. Instead, they remain active in the world, as the Buddha did, helping others to extinguish suffering by sharing their insights.

A particularly noble Buddhist tradition flourished in Tibet until that culture was crushed by its ancient antagonist, China, in 1959. (Tibetan Buddhism continues to flourish under the guidance of the current Dalai Lama, "superior priest," in Northern India.) Before Buddhism, Tibet was a warrior society that was obsessed with devils and practiced a shaman religion called Bon. After Buddhism became mixed with Bon, this warlike society became internationally known for its pervasive religiosity, charity, gentleness, and compassion.

One of the longest-lasting debates in Indian philosophy, one that in many ways anticipated the debates about faith and reason in Western philosophy, concerns the role of the intellect (as opposed to mystical experience) in the attainment of enlightenment or liberation. In order to attain Nirvana, it is first essential to free oneself from illusion, and in particular the illusion of one's special place in the world. The ground of enlightenment can be best prepared, according to many Buddhists, with a healthy dose of logic. With logical analysis, our ordinary, common-sense understanding of ourselves and the world can be shown to be utterly confused and contradictory. One of the obstacles to enlightenment is the illusion of understanding, and the play of paradoxes is the key to unlocking this illusion.

The single most famous practitioner of this play of paradoxes was the Buddhist philosopher *Nagarjuna* (second century B.C.E.). Nagarjuna was the founder of the Madhyamaka, or the Middle Way School of Mahayana Buddhist philosophy, and one of the most diabolically clever "dialecticians" in the history of philosophy. In his principal *Fundamental Verses on the Middle Way,* he launched a scathing attack on essentialism and substantialism in all forms, deriving the interdependence of phenomena and their emptiness of any essence or identity apart from convention. He articulated and defended a doctrine of two truths—a conventional truth about everyday phenomena, and the ultimate truth that these things are "empty" of the independent identity they appear to have. His deepest insight was that these two truths are at bottom the same.

Nagarjuna used the intellect against itself, arguing, for instance, that as every attempted justification invites the demand for another justification, the result is an endless regress that provides no justification at all. He developed a theory about the nature of emptiness, clearing the way to pure (but not, therefore, uninformed or unlearned) mystical experience. By emphasizing the practices of Buddhism rather than intellectual understanding, Nagarjuna expressed what he considered the true message of the Buddha. And, not coincidentally, he saw in his own cleverness a manifestation of wisdom, one of the Buddha's essential "perfections," the mark of a Bodhisattva.

Buddhist logic became increasingly rich in succeeding centuries, spurred in part by attempts to refute Nagarjuna on logical grounds. In the next millennium, there would be a virtual festival of Indian philosophy, often combative, often brilliant. In particular, the realist tradition called *Nyaya* ("logic") would become an influential counterbalance to the "illusionism" of many Vedantins and skeptics. The *Nyayayikas* rejected the notion that the everyday world was an illusion. The world, they insisted, was real. The *Nyayayikas* also believed in God, but God was not very important in their conception of the world. Accordingly, they had doubts about the emphasis on mysticism and the religious orientation assumed by most Indian philosophers.

In Tibet, mysticism and Mahayana Buddhism would have a long and glorious history. Tsong Khapa (1357–1419 C.E.) would become the founder of the most politically powerful of the four principal Tibetan schools. In his *Great Exposition of the Stages of the Path*, he provided an encyclopedia of Buddhist philosophy comparable in scope and importance to the comprehensive works of Aristotle or Thomas Aquinas. Tsong Khapa is best known for his exposition and defense of Nagarjuna and his synthesis of the metaphysics of emptiness, logic, and epistemology. His greatest philosophical achievement was his demonstration of the centrality of the philosophy of language to Buddhist philosophy.

In Search of Harmony: Confucius, Taoism, and Mo

We have noted that philosophy in China can best be summarized by the word *harmony*. Confucius focused on the ethical and social conduct that would be conducive to a harmonious community. The original Taoists, by contrast, were reclusive individuals who saw society as harmful and urged harmony in nature and within one's own nature. Lao Tzu ackowledged the desirability of social harmony, but he considered such harmony more likely to prevail if society were ruled by sages, wise men who had first found harmony within themselves. Indeed, according to the Taoists, such "rulers" need not rule, for the wise ruler is one who rules as little as possible.

Confucius, on the other hand, saw his philosophy as first of all a philosophy for rulers. He often used music and the harmony of voices as an analogy: the wise ruler, he says, will harmonize society. Nevertheless, the harmony of society depends on individual virtue, not only in the ruler but in every member of society as well. Confucius' philosophy, accordingly, is largely an exhortation to virtue.

This emphasis on personal virtue within the context of a harmonious society is extremely important for understanding Chinese philosophy. It also provides an important link with the West. Two centuries later, in Greece, Aristotle would develop a similar conception of ethics, in which personal virtue was primary but was understood in the context of one's role in a harmoniously functioning community. (A century or so after that, the Greek and Roman Stoics would develop a concept of harmony with nature that resembled the ideas of the Taoists.) The primary importance given to virtue might be contrasted, on the other hand, with the primary importance given to the law in Judaism (which is *not* to say, of course, that Judaism does not also have a strong conception of virtuous character, or that Greek and Chinese philosophy do not recognize the importance of law).

The differences between the two visions of society and the individual which are indicated by the emphases on personal virtue and on law are significant. Jewish law presumes the presence of an all-powerful God who both dictated the laws and sanctions them, while both the Greeks and the Chinese saw the sole end of ethics as the promotion of a harmonious society, quite apart from any external judge or law-giver. Confucius did refer to the will of heaven (*t' ien*); but this is usually interpreted as a reminder that while human beings can influence their circumstances, they cannot control them or assure their success or failure. In this respect, too, Confucianism can be compared and contrasted with Greek thought, with its emphasis on human vulnerability to fate.

For Confucius, the single most important virtue in any society is good leadership. Good leadership requires the personal development of the ruler, who in turn inspires virtue in his subjects. The Confucian emphasis on self-realization should be understood in this social context. It is not individual enlightenment or personal perfection; it is through and through a *social* concern. By comparison, Judaism, Christianity, and Islam tend to be more individualistic, more concerned with the well-being of the individual soul (Christianity especially so). In Confucianism, there is no atomistic "soul" in the Western sense, for the individual cannot be distinguished from his or her social roles and relationships, especially relationships within the *family*. Society as a whole, in Confucian thought, is like a gigantic extended family, even such an enormous society as China.

The key Confucian virtue, encompassing other virtues within it, is *jen* (pronounced "ren"), which can be translated as "humanity" or "humaneness." Although Confucius believed that *jen* is inherent in human beings, he insisted that becoming a full human being is an achievement. *Jen* must be cultivated and developed. In a child, *jen* is developed by observing filial piety, behavior in accordance with respect for one's parents. In a young adult, *jen* is manifested as more general social respect and piety. An important manifestation of *jen*,

accordingly, is *li*, or ritual. Li involves more than the external observance of ceremonial forms; it requires an active sense of appropriateness to one's context, as well as grace and feeling in one's actions.
Disciplined physical exercise, another virtue, is understood as a means
of attaining spiritual mastery over oneself. Mind and body are not
opposites. Both are expressions of *ch'i*, or "energy." Ceremony and
music are particularly important to the Confucians, for not only do
they bring society together, but they provide the rituals through
which *jen* is learned, practiced, and cultivated.

NOT ALL OF Confucius' immediate successors were satisfied with
the emphases and omissions in his philosophy. Mo Tzu (c. 479–381
B.C.E.), whose life began at approximately the time Confucius'
ended, was critical of Confucius for his endorsement of existing
institutions. Mo Tzu objected to the position of the aristocracy and
contended that rituals and ceremonies were unimportant. The ethical
ideal of the good society could be achieved only by means of **universal love**. Somewhat paradoxically, the Mohists also developed the art
of military strategy. The apparent paradox is resolved, however, if one
accepts the claim that Mo Tzu and his school opposed aggressive war
and considered military force warranted only for purposes of self-
defense, a position reiterated by the great strategist Sun Tzu in his
classic *Art of War*. Love may be the answer, but its precondition is
security backed up by force.

Against Mo Tzu, the Confucians responded that universal love was
impossible and undesirable. It is quite appropriate, they said, that
one's love for one's parents be greater than one's love for strangers.
Mencius (371–289 B.C.E.) contended that in order for love to be
more than superficial, it must admit of gradations. Love for humanity
at large may be an extension of the more powerful love one feels for
one's own family. Contending that human beings are essentially good,
Mencius was optimistic about humanity's ability to be benevolent,
although he considered training and commitment to be essential.

The Confucian school was not in agreement, however, about
whether human beings are inherently good. Hsün Tzu (c. 298–238
B.C.E.) contended just the opposite. Human beings, in his view, are
naturally evil, with innate tendencies to pursue personal gain and
pleasure. Fortunately, however, human beings are also intelligent, and
with their intelligence they can cultivate themselves and become
good. In keeping with the doctrines of Confucius, Hsün Tzu stressed

the importance of ritual and appropriate behavior, particularly toward members of one's family. Family relationships are not grounded in nature; instead, they are inventions of human intelligence to ensure social cooperation in the face of our more natural selfish desires. In contemporary terminology, Hsün Tzu's claim is that kinship and social relationships are socially constructed. In the debate about the relative merits of culture and nature, therefore, Hsün Tzu consistently sides with culture against nature. In this respect, his position is in adamant opposition to the teachings of Taoism.

Lao Tzu's philosophy was primarily focused on the means of achieving wisdom by tuning the inner person to the rhythms of nature, the Tao, the Way of the universe. Where the Confucians put their emphasis on society, Lao Tzu downplayed the social and stressed the importance of spontaneity in accordance with one's own nature. Simplicity, the avoidance of artificiality, is the Taoist way to wisdom. In this view, even traditional moral concepts like good and evil can be obstacles to living in accordance with the Tao. Too often such concepts are understood so rigidly that they obscure more than they illuminate; and they fail, in particular, to reflect the subtle changes of the Tao.

According to Lao Tzu, the greatest virtue is non-action (*wu-wei*). The ideal leader, accordingly, does not actively lead. According to the Taoist *Chuang Tzu* (c. 369–286, a contemporary of Mencius), governments are obstacles to human happiness, which depends on humans' individual freedom to spontaneously express the nature within them. Similarly, the ideal teacher does not teach. Avoiding all unnecessary effort, the wise person "acts naturally," behaving spontaneously in accordance with nature. He or she adopts a stance of receptiveness and expresses the Way of the universe (the universal Tao) to achieve *Te*, a person's own natural virtue.

Taoists believe that to be wise is to realize one's unity with nature and to live in conjunction with nature's rhythm, the Tao. Life and death are merely aspects of this rhythm, so the importance of life and death should not be overemphasized. The Tao's rhythm is cyclical. Every condition that is manifest at any given time gives way to other conditions, eventually to return. (The cyclical notion of "eternal recurrence" was essential to Hindu philosophy. It was also part of archaic Greek thought, but it lost favor with the beginnings of Western philosophy.) Eventually, a sage will identify only with the Tao and will "forget" the distinction between self and Tao. In this mystical condition, the sage achieves eternal life. The personal self of the sage may die, but the Tao with which the sage identifies lives on.

The Taoist interest in cycles of change is reflected in the complementary notions of *yin* and *yang*, literally "the dark side" and "the sunny side," which can be used to describe any play of opposites within change. Deficiency in any quality (yin) gives way to sufficiency (yang) and then excess, and this will be followed by decline and deficiency again. The significance of patterns of waxing and waning was so apparent to Chinese thinkers—as it was to most people in the largely agrarian China—that the complementarity of *yin* and *yang* eventually became a standard conception and an exemplary focus of wisdom throughout Chinese philosophy. The most famous of ancient Chinese texts, the *I Ching* ("Book of Changes") is seen by the Taoists as indicating intelligible moments of change within the larger flux of reality. The *I Ching* is also one of the classic texts of the Confucians.

We might compare the Taoist insistence on flow and change with the essentialism of the Judeo-Christian-Islamic tradition, which insists on the notion of *eternity* for all things sacred. Taoism has a concept of eternity, too, in the sense that the Tao's fundamental patterns endure through all changes; the Tao, in fact, is sometimes described as "the invariable" (*ch'ang*). But in Taoism one is part of nature, flowing through time. In the Judeo-Christian-Islamic tradition, by contrast, one is holy insofar as one is *not* part of nature and is *outside* of time ("in the world but not of it," in the New Testament formulation). The Christian soul, in particular, is an intact bit of eternity in everyone. The Taoist soul is more like a drop of water in a stream.

The Stuff of the World: Early Greek Philosophy

Before we attempt to review the progression of Greek philosophers prior to Socrates, we should note that the sixth and fifth centuries B.C.E. in Greece were innovative and productive in many ways. Most important was the explosion of technology. Into the midst of an essentially feudal agrarian society of wealthy landowners and peasants came a new class of craftsmen, tradesmen, and technicians. Inventors were numerous, and inventions were plentiful. The geometry and mathematics that the Greeks imported from Egypt and Babylon allowed them to make new breakthroughs in navigation and mapmaking. The science and practice of medicine flourished. The great physician Hippocrates (c. 460–377 B.C.E.) summed up the new consciousness of the age by saying, "Men think [a disease] divine merely because they do not understand it. But if they called everything divine which they do not understand, why, there would be no end of divine things."

The first Greek philosopher is usually said to be *Thales*, who lived in Asia Minor (now Turkey) in the seventh century B.C.E. (624–546) Unfortunately, we know very little about him, as we possess nothing of his writings, and what little we do know comes from the not always reliable source of Aristotle. Thales suggested that the world is surrounded by and ultimately born of water, an idea that very likely came from earlier Greek cosmogony and other cultures' ideas. Breaking with the mythological tradition that explained all of nature in terms of gods, goddesses, and other spirits, Thales adopted what we might call a *naturalistic* outlook, a scientific viewpoint—an explanation of natural phenomena in terms of other straightforward natural phenomena. His speculations were quite at home in the midst of the pragmatic explosion of innovation and technology, reflecting society's fascination with *techne*, the new way of looking at nature.

The speculations of the pre-Socratic philosophers also had a political dimension, whether or not this is evident in what remains of their works. It was during the sixth century of Greek history that Solon "modernized" Athens and established democracy. After Solon, Athens would return to tyranny, experience a devastating invasion by Sparta, and suffer a local revolution. Democracy reappeared later, but this was not, as we would like to believe, an easy or peaceful process. We must place the first philosophers within this often violent context if we are to understand their passion for order and understanding.

Thales was taken to task by his younger contemporary *Anaximander* (610–545 B.C.E.), who rejected his elder's view of a world made of water and suggested a different vision. Anaximander organized traditional Greek cosmology, distinguishing earth, air, fire, and water, and explained how their various properties—the hot and the cold, the wet and the dry—acted upon and opposed one another. (We might note here another critical point of contrast between Greek and Chinese philosophy. Opposition is often basic to Greek philosophy, whereas the Chinese would rather talk about "harmony.")

Pressed for an answer to Thales' question about which of the elements was most basic, Anaximander's answer was, "none of those." The ultimate source of the universe and the basic ingredient of all things, he said, is something we cannot perceive. He called it *apeiron*, which we might just call "basic stuff," although the word in Greek means "unbounded" or "unlimited." In terms of the history of science, this is perhaps the first significant instance of an inference to a theoretical postulate, something purported to exist in order to explain perceivable phenomena although it is not perceivable itself. (Electrons and genes are more recent examples.)

Anaximenes was a student of Anaximander. He criticized his teacher's mysterious and unperceivable *apeiron* and moved back into the realm of ordinary experience. Accordingly, Anaximenes argued that air was the most essential of the elements, condensing and evaporating, heating up and cooling off, thickening and thinning.

Thales, Anaximander, and Anaximenes—"the Milesians,"—made a major move beyond the old mythologies and folktales of Greece. Yet we should be cautious about describing this change in terms of such loaded notions as "philosophy" and "rationality." The Milesians set the stage for what we have come to call philosophy as well as much of what we have come to call science. But it is against the background of Thales, Anaximander, and Anaximenes that we can appreciate the far more radical departures of their successors.

THALES, ANAXIMANDER, AND Anaximenes were all *materialists*: the world, for each of them, was made up of some basic kind of stuff, whether it be water or air or *apeiron*. **Pythagoras** (571–497 B.C.E.), by contrast, insisted that the basic ingredients of the cosmos were numbers and proportions—not "stuff" at all, but rather forms and relationships. It is *order as such* that claims our philosophical attention, he said, not the material ordered. (This is, of course, a view very sympathetic to many physicists working today, who insist that mathematics is the key to understanding the universe.) It is with Pythagoras in particular that the central question of ontology, the study of being, becomes focused: How does the abstract order or form of things manifest itself in the multitude of actual things in the world? This is sometimes summarized as "the Problem of the One and the Many."

Mathematics, as the Greeks soon appreciated, differed from all other forms of knowledge. It possessed an elegance, a purity, an attractive universality, and a certainty that were to be found nowhere else, especially in the messy business of everyday life. The propositions of mathematics and geometry were true, true everywhere, and they could be proved for certain. A right triangle in Egypt or Persia had exactly the same formal properties as a right triangle in Athens or Italy. The proof of the Pythagorean Theorem was valid not here or there, but everywhere. Ever since Pythagoras, the elegance, purity, and certainty of mathematics have remained an ideal for many philosophers, the ultimate demonstration of rationality at its best, a systematic display of the abstract forms so loved by pure thinkers.

Pythagoras was a mesmerizing philosopher who used his theory of proportions to explain, among other things, the nature of music and the movements of the stars. He surmised that the stars made a great deal of noise (audible only to the gods), which he called "the music of the spheres." Most important of all, Pythagoras developed a complex vision of the soul, the afterlife and the right way to live. He defended the ("Eastern") belief in reincarnation. And it is worth mentioning that, in the male-chauvinist atmosphere of ancient Greece, Pythagoras included among his many followers the first women philosophers, who joined him in his thoughtful, highly intellectual search for the spiritual life. Plato, in *The Republic*, would praise Pythagoras as one who "presided over a band of intimate disciples who loved him for the inspiration of his society and handed down a way of life which to this day distinguishes the Pythagoreans from the rest of the world." Indeed, Plato himself, by some accounts, was an unacknowledged but devout Pythagorean.

Because he was a cult figure and because his members were very successful in keeping their secrets, we do not know much about Pythagoras or his teachings. We do know that he was the first thinker to actually call himself a "philosopher," that is, a "lover of wisdom." When asked if he were a wise man, Pythagoras humbly replied, "No, I am only a lover of wisdom." Such humility has not always been evident in the history of the passion for wisdom.

ALSO IN CONTRAST to the Miletian materialists, we can appreciate the murky but monumental philosophy of *Heraclitus* (536–470 B.C.E.). The "dark sayings" of Heraclitus are virtually unmatched in philosophy for their puzzling profundity and ambiguity (for instance, "The way up and the way back are the same.") While other philosophers were trying to get to the bottom of nature, Heraclitus announced that "nature loves concealment." He himself loved puzzles, paradoxes, and puzzling word play that concealed his own meanings. He suggested, to the irritation of his contemporaries, that nature makes itself known only to very few. And while he taught that there was an underlying order to the world, a *logos* that moves through all things, he kept telling his colleagues that they would "never understand it."

Heraclitus was content to be viewed in the traditional role of the sage, the prophet, the wise man, a human version of the oracle. Yet Heraclitus could also be viewed as an early philosopher-scientist who embraced yet another of the natural elements, fire. In many ways, he speaks of fire in the same sort of way that the materialists had talked about water, air, and *apeiron*. He saw lightning (thunderbolts) as divine and fire as their underlying stuff: "Fire lives the death of earth and our lives the death of fire." But the element of fire played a **symbolic** role in Heraclitus's thought that the other elements did not play for the Milesians.

Fire is violent. A flame is constantly changing, flickering. For Heraclitus, the world was constantly changing, "in flux," and apparent stability was an illusion. It was Heraclitus who insisted, famously, that one cannot step in the same river twice. (What he actually said was, "Upon those who step into the same rivers, different and again different waters flow.") But the language of Heraclitus is so metaphorical that it is impossible to think of him as merely another materialist. He was making a much larger (and very Eastern) point—that the constant in the universe appears to be change. And yet, the world is eternal and connected in a single unity by the *logos*. Here we can see an important continuity with Anaximander, the postulation of the unseen, but the *logos* is not just another kind of stuff. According to the philosophers, the difference between the way the world appears to be, in our ordinary view of things, and the way it really is was greater than ever.

Parmenides was an extremely difficult thinker who also lived in the fifth century (515–450 B.C.E.). It is with him that the philosophical abyss between reality and appearance reached its greatest extreme. Parmenides argued in a more abstract way than any of his predecessors or contemporaries and invented what he announced was a "new way of thinking." He was not concerned with the particular composition of things, like his scientific predecessors; he was interested in "being as such." He shifted the emphasis in ontology to a new level of abstraction having much to do with the most fundamental aspects of [Greek] language, notably the verb *to be*. (Let us pass over the fact that not all languages have the verb *to be* or anything much like it.) Looking back to the arguments of his predecessors and playing with paradoxes, Parmenides argued the striking thesis that the world as we "know" it is not the true world, even though we cannot know any other.

Whatever is must be eternal; it cannot come into being, and it cannot be destroyed. From this, Parmenides concludes that there can be no such thing as change. But what we ordinarily experience, as Heraclitus had also insisted, was constant change. What we call reality, therefore, is nothing but "the deceitful ordering of words." The true reality, on the other hand, is absolutely unitary, unchanging, eternal, "the one." (It is worth noting that Vedantins were proposing similar arguments about change and permanence around the same time.)

Immediately after Parmenides, there were only so many ways for philosophers to respond. One way, of course, was simply to agree with him, and this is what his student Zeno did. *Zeno* invented a series of ingenious arguments to "prove" that, indeed, the very notions of time and change were utter nonsense. The most famous of these were a group of paradoxes, in the form of arguments "to absurdity" (*reductio ad absurdum*), whose point was to show that, if one assumes that time or change is real, then nonsense follows. Therefore, there can be no time or change. The most familiar of these paradoxes is perhaps the paradox of the arrow. If an arrow moves from bow to target, it must traverse some portion of its trajectory. But to do that, it must traverse some smaller portion, and to do that, some smaller portion, and so on *ad infinitum*, and therefore it never reaches its target. The tricks and sleights necessarily involved in such "proofs" need not detain us here. Suffice it to say that they perplexed many of the philosophers in the fourth century B.C.E. who were challenged to try to refute them.

ONE OF THOSE who felt so challenged was *Democritus* (460–370 B.C.E.). His strategy was to undermine the premises of Parmenides' and Zeno's arguments and, at the same time, to further develop the scientific cosmology of the Milesians. One of those premises, which Parmenides and Zeno simply took over from the earlier pre-Socratics, was their "monism," their assumption that reality must be a unity. Democritus, by contrast, was a "pluralist"—he rejected the idea that the world was based on any one element or unified by any one order.

Democritus pursued the idea of smaller and smaller pieces of "stuff" until he landed upon what would later become one of the most important ideas of modern times, the concept of the *atom*. Democritus was an extreme pluralist in his belief that the world consisted of any number of various "particles," differing in sizes and shapes but, as elements, having one distinctive feature in common.

These particles could not be cut or further divided. (The word "atom" implies this, for it stems from *a*, not, and *tom*, cut.) Directly contradicting Parmenides, Democritus declared that all that exists is atoms, moving in the void. Yet every atom is eternal and can be neither created nor destroyed.

With Democritus, the attempt to deanimate and demythologize the world was complete. He imagined the universe as thoroughly material, devoid of any imposed order or intelligence, devoid of an underlying *logos* or purpose. The old ideas about fate controlling our destiny, about gods and goddesses ruling the world, even the idea of a soul or psyche surviving us after death—all of this disappeared. Democritus developed a purely materialist theory of the world as devoid of spirits and animation. Even the human soul, a matter of mystery to most of the pre-Socratics, was for Democritus just one more material atom in a universe of material atoms.

The *soul* has been one of the recurring themes throughout the history of philosophy. It might be appropriate to summarize briefly the fate of the soul, as we have encountered it so far. In early Greek philosophy the soul was considered just another thing, and a pretty insubstantial thing at that. It had no moral significance. Indeed, the Greeks believed that the soul is rather pathetic, a source of life only when it is embodied. Otherwise, it is like a shadow, insubstantial, a mere "breath" (the original meaning of the word *psyche*). A similar view led the ancient Egyptians, in particular, to insist that a soul could enter the afterlife only if the body were preserved. They took great pains to ensure bodily preservation of the dead (and to accompany the body with all of its accoutrements, luxuries, and servants). This practice of preservation suggests why the early Christians came to take the resurrection of the body to be essential to eternal life. Heraclitus, one of the most imaginative early Greek philosophers, suggested that the soul was "fiery" and made up of the same stuff as the stars (but lest we find this view too elevated, we should remind ourselves that Heraclitus thought of the stars as mere pockets in the sky, not very substantial).

The ancient Hebrews talked very little of the abstract soul as such, more or less restricting their concern to the concrete character of the individual human being. So, too, the Chinese spoke of the "soul" of a person with only his or her personal character and social identity in mind, not with any abstract metaphysical remainder. Buddhists believed that the soul was either one with the rest of the universe or an illusion to be overcome. The Jains, by contrast, did believe in the individual soul, and that even insects and vermin had souls that were eternal. Hindus were divided on such matters, but they too believed in the continuity of the soul after death, through reincarnation or rebirth.

We should not be surprised to find that many thinkers (and most ordinary people) felt an enormous loss facing the stark, virtually soulless philosophy of Democritus. Before Christianity was even a glimmer on the horizon, and before the three greatest philosophers of Athens came on the scene, the spiritual poverty of philosophy was already a matter of concern. Indeed, one recent German philosopher has gone so far as to declare that our ability to truly philosophize was lost sometime soon after the fifth century B.C.E.

How Should We Live? Socrates and the Sophists

Suggestions that there is nothing but matter or that the world of our daily experience is an illusion obviously set philosophers against common sense in a most dramatic way. A new generation of philosophers agreed that such conclusions were unacceptable, and some of them, called *Sophists* (from *sophistes*, "practitioners of wisdom"), used the new techniques of argumentation to belittle and parody Parmenides' philosophy. Others exploited the skepticism about our ever knowing the truth and used Parmenides' arguments to advance radical ideas in religion and morality. Such ideas included the suggestion that all human knowledge and values are merely "relative" and not ultimately "true" at all. In ethics, it was similarly argued that our ideals are in fact nothing more than the ideals of those who rule, and that justice is nothing but the advantage of those already in power. (In other words, "might makes right.") Other Sophists simply taught the techniques of argumentation, coaching eager and ambitious young Athenians on how to win arguments, score points, tie their opponents in verbal knots, impress the public, and make political careers for themselves in the new democracy.

With the sophists, in other words, philosophy became thoroughly *practical*, a way of making one's way in the world. Enough about the origins of the world and the nature of ultimate reality. Enough dark sayings and impossible arguments. Let's get down to the business of living, of using philosophy to make something of ourselves and, not to be too disrespectful, to have a little fun.

Among the various Sophists, we might mention *Gorgias* (483–376 B.C.E.), who imitated Parmenides' new style of argument and "proved" that (a) nothing exists, (b) if anything did exist, it would be unintelligible, and (c) if something were intelligible, one could say nothing about it. It seems reasonable to interpret these propositions and arguments as they were probably intended—as a parody, and as a demonstration not of the absurd conclusions themselves but that this whole business of "proofs" is really just nonsense. Given sufficiently abstruse, arcane, or ambiguous premises and a good deal of cleverness, a smart philosopher can "prove" just about anything. In the clash of conflicting claims about the world beyond our experience, there is no ultimate proof or demonstration, only rhetoric and opinion, more or less skillfully presented.

Perhaps the most famous Sophist was *Protagoras* (490–420 B.C.E.), who said that "man is the measure of all things." This is sometimes quoted as an early statement of pragmatism, the view that we should believe what is useful to us. It also suggests a kind of skepticism, that is, a pervasive and irrefutable reason for doubting all claims about reality beyond our own human perspective. "Man is the measure" on this view means that knowledge is relative to human beings and limited to their viewpoint, and that this viewpoint does not allow us to know things as they are in themselves.

There is a less skeptical way of interpreting Protagoras, however, so that his statement becomes a statement of confidence rather than doubt. In this interpretation, we know the world *because* we view it in human terms. The implications of this view would not be worked out for another two thousand years, but suffice it to say for now that the philosophy of Protagoras the Sophist does not have to be read as "sophistry," in the narrow sense of argument for its own sake. It can be interpreted as a keenly insightful view into the nature of knowledge. As a response to Parmenides, it relocates the concern about ultimate reality to questions of human knowledge.

AGAINST SUCH "SOPHISTRIES," the philosopher *Socrates* (470–399 B.C.E.) argued that there were, in fact, real and "objective" values, and that reason could be used not only to win arguments but to discover the most important truths about human life. Like the other Sophists, he excelled in logical as well as rhetorical tricks and twists, many of them borrowed from the ingenious Parmenides and the exceedingly clever Zeno. Socrates knew how to make a seeming truism collapse in on itself in paradox, how to turn a platitude into a contradiction, how to twist an argument so that its sharpest barbs pointed back at its propounder. He knew how to counter any generalization with "counterexamples" and ask the hardest questions, promote the most provocative theories, and parody the most respectable lines of argument until they were reduced to nonsense, or worse.

Socrates' point, however, was not just to demolish other people's claims and arguments, even though he rarely gave the answers to his own questions. His point was to force others to seek the answers themselves, and Socrates, unlike some of the Sophists, seemed confident that there was, in fact, an answer to the basic questions about life. The truth be told, Socrates was not opposed to the Sophists; he was the best of them. Although he was the first to admit his own ignorance, he also believed in something. Socrates believed that virtue is the most valuable of all possessions, that the truth lies beyond the "shadows" of our everyday experience, and that it is the proper business of the philosopher to show us how little we really know. But like the clever logicians of ancient India, his demonstrations of ignorance were preparatory to true knowledge, which, as in India, had to be "seen," not merely learned.

Socrates would etch a vivid representation of "the philosopher" into the consciousness of the West. But whatever his virtues, and they were many, he owes his unique place in Western thinking to a fate both tragic and happy. In 399 B.C.E., Socrates was brought to trial, charged with "corrupting the minds" of his students, and famously condemned and executed. It was no doubt one of democratic Athens's most trying and embarrassing moments. But it established Socrates not only as a philosopher but as a martyr for the truth, for his calling. "I would rather die than give up philosophy," he announced to the jury, virtually demanding his own execution. Socrates set the standards for what philosophy should be, and they were very high standards indeed.

Socrates did not write anything. He did not put his ideas in to thematic order, nor is it evident that he had anything like a philosophical system. In many ways, he could be said to be in the same tradition as the Old Testament prophets, and he is often compared to Jesus. He was a sage, a wiseman, a "gadfly." He argued his philosophy personally and publicly in the marketplace of Athens. Socrates thought that his fellow citizens, especially those uneducated democrats who thought they knew so much, were virtual morons. He took it upon himself to make sure that they knew this. He asked them such questions as: What is virtue? What is knowledge? What is justice? He deftly demonstrated both the difficulty of these philosophical queries and the doltishness of his democratic colleagues.

But it was Socrates' happy fate to be blessed with a student who was perhaps one of the most brilliant writers in the history of humanity. Plato was an excellent student, an ardent admirer, a keen listener, a witty journalist, a skilled propagandist, an accomplished dramatist, and a philosophical genius in his own right. Plato first recorded, then elaborated, then embellished and transformed Socrates' many conversations, beginning with the circumstances of his trial. The resulting dialogues are the first full body of work we have in philosophy, and they are such astounding documents that it has been famously noted that all of (Western) philosophy is nothing but a footnote to Plato.

Nevertheless, Plato remains quietly in the background; Socrates is the hero of the dialogues. If it were not for Plato, of course, Socrates would be little but a footnote in the archives of Greek history. But if it were not for Socrates we probably would have no Plato, and without Plato no Aristotle, through whom we know most of what we know about the philosophers who preceded Socrates. The "miracle" of Greek philosophy might never have happened.

The Philosopher's Philosophers: Plato and Aristotle

Plato (427–347) was the greatest writer in Western philosophy and a genius of a dramatist. Of course, he was fortunate to have his work survive. Plato also founded a school, the Academy, to make sure that his writings and ideas (and the teachings of Socrates) were kept alive. Compared to virtually any philosopher after him, Plato was more brilliant, more moving, funnier, and more profound. The fate of Socrates overshadowed every Platonic dialogue, lending poignance to every exchange and giving dignity to every argument. Indeed, the use of Socrates, first as the dramatic hero but later on as a philosophical mouthpiece, was so successful that Plato continued using him even when it became clear that the ideas supposedly being articulated and argued by Socrates were actually Plato's own.

Plato's philosophy began with a credible if overly admiring and uncritical account of Socrates, particularly Socrates' last days. Socrates' trial, imprisonment, and execution are reported in the *Apology*, the

Crito, and the *Phaedo,* respectively. Plato also recorded extensive con-versations — dialogues — in which Socrates holds forth with some of the cleverest (and a few not-so-clever) thinkers of his time, including Parmenides, Protagoras, and Gorgias. Through Socrates' refutation of their various arguments, Plato begins to suggest his own views. Plato's cosmological concerns include the Pythagorean view of the world as number, the Heraclitean view of the world as flux and as *logos,* and the Parmenidean vision of an eternal, unchanging, unknowable reality.

Central to Plato's philosophy, at most implied by Socrates, was his theory of Forms. This theory entailed a "two-world" cosmology. One world is our everyday world of change and impermanence. The other is an ideal world populated by ideal "Forms." The first, the "world of becoming," was in flux, as Heraclitus insisted, but the latter, the "World of Being," was eternal and unchanging, as Parmenides demanded.

What made Plato's new vision so appealing was that, first of all, the two worlds were interrelated, not unrelated as Parmenides and some of the Sophists had argued. The world of becoming, our world, was defined by ("participated in") a World of Being, the world of ideal Forms. The Forms were the perfect models, the ideal being, of every kind of thing. Thus the idea of an unchanging *logos* underlying the everyday world could be understood as the ideality of the Forms, defining the world despite the fact of continual change. Furthermore, this ideal world of Forms was not, as in Parmenides, unknowable. According to Plato, we could get at least a glimpse of this world through reason.

Perhaps the most memorable image of the Forms and their ability to dazzle the philosopher who sees them is the vision that Plato describes for us in his masterpiece, *The Republic.* There he spins "The Myth of the Cave," which is both an allegory concerning the rela-tionship between the World of Being and the world of becoming — the Forms and the things of this world — and a warning of the dangers facing the philosopher. The Myth begins with the image of a number of slaves shackled in a cave with their faces to the wall. What they see, and what they consider to be reality, are the shadows cast on the wall. So, too, Socrates goes on to explain (as he narrates the alle-gory), what we all take to be reality consists ultimately of shadows. It is not that these are unreal — they are real shadows — but they are shadows of things that are even more real. So the distinction here is not, as in Parmenides, between reality and illusion. It is the distinc-tion between the more and less real, a superior and an inferior world.

Now suppose that one of the slaves, a philosopher, were to break free and turn around, casting his eyes for the first time on the genuine objects that cast the shadows, and then move out of the cave into the bright light of the sun. Would he not be dazzled? Would he not immediately see how imperfect are the shadows of everyday reality compared with the reality he now observed? So, too, the philosopher is dazzled when he sees the perfect Forms of virtue, justice, and courage compared to the imperfect and usually confused ideas and actions of ordinary men and women. How much "higher" his aspirations would then be. And if this philosopher were then to turn back to the cave and try to tell his fellows how impoverished their world was, how inadequate their ideals, would they not turn on him and kill him? The reference to Socrates' own fate is unmistakable, but the allusion to the Forms is of much more general and profound significance.

The theory of Forms makes Plato's philosophy sound very abstract and cosmological. In fact, it was first of all a practical philosophy, and the *Republic* was a political and very polemical book. The republic described by Plato had much in common, needless to say, with the Athenian city-state, but it also displayed some disconcerting differences, many of which we still find extreme. To begin with, it was not a democracy. On this point, Plato and Socrates are certainly in agreement. They believed that rule should be in the hands of those who know best and have insight into virtue — philosophers. In the *Republic* Plato gives us the image of philosopher-kings, which was no doubt received with as much ridicule then as now. (The absent-minded-philosopher joke had been around at least since Thales.)

Plato's republic is oddly authoritarian, hierarchical, and egalitarian in turns. It is a "natural" aristocracy, based on talent, the fortunes of birth and upbringing. It is a benign dictatorship in which everyone, including the "guardians," knows their place. It is not a society that caters to individuals or to individual interests, but one in which the individual and individual interests are subordinated to the common good. Plato advocates the use of artistic censorship, the banning of subversive poetry, for example, contending that the stimulating influence of art should be limited to the role of instilling appropriate social attitudes and behavior. His is a society in which people are not entitled to own property and are not even free to bring up their own children, who are educated instead by the state. But it is a society in which women are to be given as much power as men, a daring suggestion in those times. The well-being of the least citizen is to be considered as important as that of the greatest. Even the rulers are given no special privileges and are not expected to be especially happy, given their awesome responsibilities. Happiness, Plato tells us, is not for any privileged class of citizens but for the city-state as a whole.

It is difficult to reconcile this anti-democratic vision of the good society and Socrates' almost saintly example of the good but eccentric gadfly. But the *Republic* is not just a political model of an imagined state. It also advocates a new way of thinking about ourselves and the world. We might reject the authoritarian and inegalitarian aspects of the republic described without dismissing the *Republic*'s worldview. So, too, we might reject the metaphysical extreme of believing in another world of absolute ideals without letting go of the ideal of virtuousness and the importance of the cultivation of the virtues. But Plato, following Socrates, had something more to promise us than a utopian city-state and a rather incredible metaphysics. He also gave us an inspiring picture of the soul, which now had to navigate an entirely new way of looking at the world.

As we mentioned earlier, the Greeks, from Homer to Democritus, "believed in" the soul only to a minimal extent. They admitted that something, call it "breath," was needed to animate the body, and that it departed the body with death. But according to this picture, the soul needed the body just as much as the body needed the soul. Without the soul, the body was dead, but without the body, the soul was just a pathetic shadow with no meaning and no value. For Socrates and Plato, on the other hand, the soul took on moral significance. It became both independent of and more important than the body. In the *Apology*, Socrates fantasizes about the joy of thinking philosophy all of the time in the afterlife, without interruptions or distractions. It was as if he faced death as the prospect of a long vacation, even as a cure. That is why, according to Socrates, a truly good man can ultimately suffer no evil, despite physical harm or even death.

Moreover, if the soul belongs (in part) to the World of Being, then it already contains the knowledge of the Forms. Thus, our knowledge of virtue, beauty, and the good does not depend on learning, much less being taught about them; we are born with this knowledge. It is "innate" (literally, "born into" us). In the *Phaedo*, Socrates says, "In order to know anything absolutely, we must be free from the body and behold actual reality with the eyes of the soul alone." The soul thus becomes the conduit of intellectual as well as moral life. Quite literally, it is the one thing in life truly worth worrying about.

AS A STUDENT of Plato, *Aristotle* (384–322 B.C.E.) was naturally concerned with his teacher's theory of Forms, which he rejected. As the grand-student of Socrates, he was also particularly interested in his teacher's concept of the virtues, and here he could heartily agree. But this agreement could not extend to the otherworldly notion of Virtue-as-such, Virtue as an ideal Form. A virtue, according to Aristotle, is a concrete aspect of individual character, not an abstraction or an ideal detached from the people who exemplify it.

Aristotle was much more of a scientist than Plato. The sign above the door at Plato's Academy allegedly instructed all entrants to learn geometry. Aristotle's Lyceum, on the other hand, was filled with scientific exhibits, collections of rocks, plants, animal remains. Unlike earlier philosophers, Aristotle did not distrust the senses but *used* them to observe, to collect specimens, and to experiment, although it must be said that sometimes he put more faith in reason than in experience. (It was many centuries before Galileo showed that, contrary to reason—that is, Aristotle's untested expectations—a large stone falls no faster than a small stone.)

Looking back at the progress and the attempts of the pre-Socratic philosophers, Aristotle summarized the whole of science before him. He himself was a cosmologist, an astronomer, a meteorologist, a physicist, a geologist, a biologist, a psychologist, and the first logician of any importance. Many of his views on the natural sciences would still be unchallenged fifteen hundred years after his death. Accordingly, Aristotle is viewed by scientists of the last few centuries with very mixed feelings. On the one hand, he was probably the greatest scientist that ever lived. On the other hand, he eventually became an enormous obstacle to scientific progress. His views were so central to the doctrines of the all-powerful medieval church that alternative theories in science were actively discouraged for centuries.

In Aristotle, as opposed to Plato, we find a "one-world" philosophy that has its feet firmly planted on the ground. Like Plato, Aristotle's aim is to find his way through the ingenuity and obscurities of the pre-Socratic philosophers in order to develop an adequate theory of both human nature and nature in general. Like Socrates, he is centrally concerned with the cultivation of the virtues, although contrary to Socrates and in agreement with the other Sophists, Aristotle claims that these can and must be taught. They can not, however, be taught in a philosophy seminar or a book. An individual has to be raised with the virtues, trained until they become second nature. Here, as always in Aristotle, the bottom line is the concrete individual in the context of society. There is no place and no need for a theory of Forms, a theory of another world. To appeal to the Forms, Aristotle says, is to fall back on "empty words and poetic metaphors."

Aristotle, unlike some of the pre-Socratics, has no problem accepting the reality of change. At the same time, he agrees that there must be some fundamental "stuff" if knowledge of the world is to be possible. He does not feel compelled to choose, as the early pre-Socratics did, one basic element (water, air, fire, *apeiron*), nor does he feel compelled to choose between the priority of form and matter. Obviously, he says, things require both. But there is no need—or intelligible reason—to separate them, as Pythagoras and Plato did.

Although the history of philosophy has been described in terms of the dueling legacies of Plato and Aristotle, Aristotle never intended a full-scale split with Plato, his teacher and friend for twenty years. Aristotle agreed with Plato that the form of things is of the utmost importance. But Aristotle maintained that the form *of* something was also *in* the thing, what he called a **substance**. A substance is nothing other than an individual thing—a person, a rock, a horse. An *essence* is what makes a substance what it is. (If Socrates loses his hair, he is still Socrates. But if Socrates becomes a frog—not a peculiarly articulate and virtuous Socratic frog but a perfectly ordinary croaking frog—that frog is no longer Socrates.) This down-to-earth talk of individual substances and essences is central to Aristotle's philosophy, and it eliminates any need to appeal to Plato's mysterious Forms.

And yet, Aristotle's philosophy also involved a "reaching beyond," not beyond sensible experience but beyond the actual state of things. Aristotle emphasized that things also have *potential*. A seed cannot be fully understood by reference to the matter that makes it up and to its current shape and features; a seed must be considered in terms of its potential to grow into a certain sort of plant. In order to understand this potential we must understand that the plant has an internal principle, a blueprint of sorts, that can direct that development. Thus a central feature of Aristotle's philosophy is *teleology*, the purposiveness of things. Stones, to be sure, have a rather simple purpose, notably to fall to the ground whenever they have the chance. Plants and animals have increasingly complicated purposes, and so, of course, do people.

Aristotle's teleology reaches its cosmic end with his concept of God, what would later be called (without praise) "the God of the philosophers." This is the ultimate principle of all motion, "the prime mover." With Aristotle more than with any Greek before him, we get an explicit idea of God that is totally devoid of anthropomorphism, a principle rather than a person. The ultimate end of the cosmos itself, the only form that exists in itself and apart from any matter, is God, the unmoved mover, eternal and complete in itself, the purpose towards which all things strive for their potential. God is fully realized activity, the activity of pure thinking, "thought thinking itself." What such a deity has in common with the God who will reign over Christianity is a difficult and debatable question, one that continues to this day.

Aristotle's teleology had its practical application in his ethics and in his politics. Strictly speaking, there is no separating the two. As in Confucius's China, the good life—which is the focus of Aristotle's treatment of ethics—requires participation in a good society. But Aristotle's society was an aristocracy, supported by slavery. Accordingly, Aristotle's ethics is concerned primarily with the virtue and well-being of an extremely privileged class of people. And his politics, for all of its merits (he is far more democratic than Plato, for example), virtually begins with a defense of the ghastly institution of slavery. Yet in both ethics and politics Aristotle has much to say to us.

Aristotle's ethics is defined in terms of "the ends of being human." People have purposes. They not only have immediate purposes—to catch that bus, to earn a promotion on the job, to get to the top of the mountain—but an ultimate natural purpose, a purpose that, Aristotle tells us, is generally agreed to be "happiness" or, more accurately, "doing well." (The Greek word is *eudaimonia*, often translated as "doing well" or "flourishing.") Aristotle's *Nicomachean Ethics*, accordingly, is the analysis of the true nature of happiness and its essential components, notably reason and virtue. Happiness, Aristotle tells us, is really just the name for the good life—that is, for whatever sort of life fulfills our proper purpose or "function."

Happiness is not the life of pleasure, Aristotle argues. Some pleasures are degrading and humiliating, and, more important, pleasure is just an accompaniment to satisfying activity, not activity's end or goal. The good life is not defined by wealth, which is just a means to happiness, nor is it defined by honor, power and success, because such things depend on the whims of others. Happiness, properly understood, should be self-contained and complete in itself. "Some philosophers," Aristotle coyly suggests, define the Good in terms of the Forms, but Aristotle will have none of that. Again, he lays out his refutation of Plato's theory.

Aristotle characterizes happiness as *the life of virtuous activity in accordance with reason.* A good life is an active life. A good life is filled with friends. ("No one would choose to live without friends.") It is a life of participation in the community. It is also a life occupied with the philosophical activity of contemplation.

The most important activities that Aristotle recommends are those that are expressions of the virtues. It is important to note that the Greek word for virtue (*arete*) can also be translated as "excellence," and a virtue is one of those traits of character that make a person excel. The virtues that occupy Aristotle's attention are those that make a person an excellent human being, such as courage, temperance, a sense of justice, a good sense of humor, truthfulness, friendliness and, in general, just being someone who is good to live with. Notice that there is nothing particularly "moral" about this list of virtues, and that neither Aristotle nor any of the other Greeks had that rather specific sense of "morality" that makes up so much of the core of ethics today. Indeed, Aristotle insists that a virtuous person *enjoys* being virtuous. There is no conflict between what one wants to do and what one ought to do, no tension between virtue and self-interest. This is more than the usual Greek plea for "moderation." Virtue involves optimum balance and measure in one's behavior, "the mean between the extremes," much as beauty involves symmetry and order.

When the Going Gets Tough: After Aristotle

The practical Romans had less love of philosophy than the more spiritual Greeks did, and Roman philosophers had their own share of tragedy. Exemplary is the fate of Seneca, one of the leading philosophers of Rome. Serving under Nero, one of a long string of corrupt and dysfunctional emperors, Seneca was ordered to commit suicide, and he did. The philosophy of the Greco-Romans was designed to cope with such tragedies and injustices, and one of its continuing themes, accordingly, was the importance of detaching oneself from the absurdities of life, through reason.

Hellenistic philosophy[3] saw the flourishing of many schools, including Neoplatonist philosophy, that would lead directly into

---

[3] "Hellenistic" historically refers to the period after Alexander the Great, but, for our purposes, it might just as well mean after Aristotle.

Christianity. There was also *Epicureanism*, founded by *Epicurus*, a follower of Democritus. Epicurus (341–270 B.C.E.) has gotten quite a reputation, which he would no doubt deplore, as the ultimate party animal. (An "Epicurean" today is a person who takes special delight in the senses, who enjoys luxury, even to excess.) What Epicurus really believed in was peace of mind (*ataraxia*). The pursuit of pleasure was perfectly "natural," but he did not encourage it, much less promote it, as the purpose of life. His main goal was freedom from anxiety, or tranquility. The wise man, said Epicurus, should have nothing to fear from life. Even death is utterly nothing, and as nothing, it is nothing to fear.

Another great Hellenistic school, *Stoicism*, was the single most successful and longest-lasting movement in Greco-Roman philosophy. Some Stoic philosophers appeared soon after Aristotle, notably Zeno (336–265 B.C.E., not to be confused with the disciple of Parmenides), and then Chryssipus (281–205 B.C.E.). Later Stoics taught during the height and then the disintegration of the Roman Empire. Their "Life is tough" theme affected not only those who were down and out, like the slave Epictetus (first century C.E.), but even those at the pinnacle of power. Indeed, one of the Stoics, Marcus Aurelius (121–180), was the Emperor of all Rome.

The Stoics can be characterized by their almost fanatic faith in reason. It is the Stoics, in particular, who intensified the ancient antagonism between reason and emotion. Emotions, the Stoics suggested, are irrational judgments that make us frustrated and unhappy. As the Buddha had taught a few centuries earlier and more than a few thousand miles to the east: Minimize your desires and you will minimize your suffering. The Stoic Epictetus (50–125) similarly declared, "Demand not that events happen as you wish, but wish them to happen as they do happen, and you will get on well."

The Stoics looked around them and found themselves in a world that had gone haywire, a social world in which vanity, cruelty, and foolishness reigned supreme. And yet, they believed in a rational universe, however irrational or absurd it may seem to human eyes. They taught that we should live "in conformity with nature," but nature was to be viewed as "in accordance with reason," not according to our feelings. Indeed, the philosophical ideal of the Stoics could be summarized as indifference, *apatheia*, apathy. Anger is pointless, they believed, and can only be self-destructive. Love and even friendship can be dangerous. The wise man forms only limited attachments and should not be afraid of tragedy or death.

Stoicism was an extreme philosophy, but one that would serve many souls well in difficult and troubled times. It became an immensely popular philosophy in Rome and throughout the Roman Empire. Indeed, the Stoics' defense of asceticism (self-denial) and faith was picked up by the early Christians and become an essential part of their philosophy as well.

Finally, there was the even more extreme philosophy of *Skepticism*, which traces itself from Pyrrho (365–275 B.C.E.) to Sextus Empiricus (second century C.E.) in Rome, who founded the school as such. Pyrrho taught that all belief is nonsense, that nothing can be known. He was famous for his recklessness—for almost wandering off cliffs, walking into horses and chariots, eating erratically, surviving thanks only to the keen watch of his friends and pupils. (Given that Pyrrho lived to be about ninety, his philosophy seems to have had its therapeutic virtues.) The Skeptics went beyond the Stoics (whom they considered "dogmatic") and argued that belief of any kind, including belief in reason, is illusory and unjustifiable. This belief too was a form of therapy, a way of detaching oneself, a way of achieving serenity and freedom from anxiety. It was quite different, therefore, from the skepticism that would flourish in modern times. For the ancient skeptics, pervasive doubt was wisdom, a reasonable way of life.

Before the "Discovery" of Africa and the Americas

Unknown to the Greeks and Romans (as much as they traveled), unknown to the Indians, the Chinese, and the great civilizations of the Middle East, there were flourishing civilizations elsewhere as well, with different ideas, different traditions, and different ways of seeing and living in the world. Some of these, notably in Meso- (middle) America, were comparable to the wonder of ancient Egypt.

The problem for historians interested in the cultures of Africa and the Americas is the absence of records. In many cases, records existed but were later destroyed, often along with the civilizations themselves. For example, the Aztecs of Mexico had a thriving school of philosophers called *tlamatinime* ("knowers of things"). But all we have left are fragments of their teachings, largely because their Spanish conquerors deliberately burned most of their books.

More problematic still are those many cultures whose literary traditions were entirely oral. When these cultures either died out or were overwhelmed by colonial conquerors, their oral traditions usually died out as well. Consequently, we do not know how long civilizations existed in the southern Americas, or when or how they developed. We do not know how ancient are the abandoned ancient cities of the central African rain forest, or how long the Navaho, Hopi, Ojibwa, Apache, Seminoles, Iroquois, and hundreds of other American Indian tribes lived in the northern Americas. There is archaeological evidence that North America was populated thousands of years ago, and it is quite clear that Africa was populated top to bottom tens of thousands of years ago. The fact that these African and American cultures seem to lack a history reflects the lack of written records rather than evidence that they had no philosophy worth noting.

What we are learning, however tentatively, about these various world cultures is, nevertheless, increasingly rich and fascinating. We can only indicate this growing awareness with a few general points here. Africa, of course, has comprised hundreds of different cultures, indeed, hundreds of different languages, but a good deal of precolonial African philosophy can be characterized by means of the twin notions of *tribalism* and a special sense of *identity with nature*.

Tribalism establishes an individual's identity and significance as a person only in the context of his or her family and community. This idea may sound striking to those in the contemporary West who have lost such familial and communitarian sensibilities to a radical individualism. But for those who live such a philosophy (and this would include the Confucian cultures of Asia as well as the many tribal societies of Africa, the Americas and the South Pacific), an isolated individual lacking the concrete presence and intangible ties of kinship is understood as hopelessly lost or effectively dead.

Traditional African tribes tend to see personhood as something achieved over time by becoming a part of one's community. As in China, ritual plays a particularly important role in this process. To become a person is an achievement. Birth and death do not mark a person's beginning and end. A newborn baby is not yet a person, while a deceased person who lives in the memory of his or her descendents is a person still, despite physical death. Initiation rites are crucial to achieving full membership in most tribal communities and thus to becoming a full person. Similarly, throughout a person's lifespan, rites and ceremonies keep his or her life in rhythm with that of the community.

The Western conception of an individual, atomic soul is alien to the thinking of most traditional Africans. In some tribes, such as the

Yoruba (now mostly in Nigeria) and the Lugbara (now mostly in Uganda), the communal basis for personhood is reflected in a conception of the human being as composed of multiple spiritual elements, all of which are essential to a person's life. In the Yoruba tribe, for instance, ancestors' souls can return in their descendents, sometimes over and over again. So far are the Yoruba from believing in an isolated individual soul that they believe that immediate descendents may be reincarnations of souls of their mothers or fathers, *even while the latter are still living*.

In light of this sense of identity, members of African tribes typically emphasize the worship of ancestors, who are considered living inhabitants of the spirit world, capable of assisting their descendents. As for the African attitude toward nature (and this would apply to many of the tribes of North America and the South Pacific as well), we need only point out that for thousands of years many Africans have accepted a philosophical perspective that we in the West are just now beginning to appreciate. In this view, human beings have not been placed here on Earth to "have dominion" over all other creatures and things, as promised in Genesis and reiterated by Francis Bacon. We are a part of the Earth, we are dependent on it, and it is dependent on us. We have ecological responsibilities; the world around us, "nature," is not just a resource or a source of aesthetic or scientific fascination. In short, we *are* nature.

We are not alone. African and American Indian tribal societies typically embrace *animism*, the belief that entities throughout nature are endowed with souls, often thought to be souls of ancestors who are no longer individually remembered. Nature, for most traditional Africans, is full of living forces. Spirits dwell within it, and human beings can interact with them to some extent, utilizing these spirits' powers or driving them elsewhere. The African conviction that human beings are intimately connected to nature is part and parcel of the traditional belief that nature is essentially spiritual.

The hunting tribes among the North American Indians acknowledged the debt that they had toward the creatures that provided their food. In their view, killing other creatures is not a right but a necessity that demands gratitude and reverence. Saying prayers and thanking one's quarry may strike most supermarket shoppers as a bit odd, but the consciousness of the fact that another creature has been killed for one's own benefit might better be seen as an essential gesture of humanity. The gesture of prayer in thanksgiving is a feature common to most American Indian traditions, reflecting a tendency to see everyday life as sacred.

To the south, the core of Meso-American philosophy was a belief in three levels of time and reality—ordinary, mythical, and divine. The mythic and divine levels of reality exerted tangible influences on the ordinary plane of human experience, and they did so at predictable times. This belief motivated detailed attention to the construction of calendars and to astronomical observation. The balance between the different orders of reality was sufficiently fragile that human beings had to assume responsibility for maintaining the cosmic order. The Mayans, the Incas, the Aztecs, and others believed that the continued existence of the universe itself depended on human actions and rituals, and in particular on the willingness of humans to sacrifice themselves. Furthermore, much as Thales and the ancient Babylonians had thought that the world was essentially water, the Mayans and the Aztecs believed that blood was the fundamental life force.

These beliefs, taken together, suggest the logic behind the best-known and most horrifying of ancient Aztec rituals: bloody human sacrifice on an enormous scale. Similarly, the Mayan kings and queens regularly pierced themselves and lost enough blood to cause them to have religious visions. They understood such relatively modest sacrifice as repayment to the gods, who had sacrificed themselves to create the world. For the Aztecs, the sacrifice was far less modest, involving wholesale killing of the best youths of their society along with captured enemies. It has been suggested that one of the reasons the warrior Aztecs lost so badly to the Spanish invaders was that, in desperation, they sacrificed so many of their best young warriors to the gods, believing that the gods had turned against them. Thus philosophy can be the undoing as well as the strength of a great civilization.

Nevertheless, despite the appalling gruesomeness that defined these rituals, the Meso-American religion contained one philosophical element famously lacking in the solemnity of the religion of the European conquistadors—an essential sense of humor. As in Hinduism and in Greece, the "jokester" (sometimes portrayed as a coyote or a fox) played an important "lightening" role in philosophy. One of the essential elements of reality, we all too easily forget, is its capacity to fool us, surprise us, and make fools out of us.

Ancient attempts to discover and master reality began to discover instead the limits of human knowledge. Nevertheless, philosophers continued to insist on transcending these limits. How would this be possible? In the West, the advent of Christianity and then Islam continued the epic debate between faith and reason, which had its early origins in the philosophies of the Hebrews and some of the more exotic theories of the Greeks. In the East, a parallel debate continued between the intellect and mystial experience. But then again, there was always the possibility that Protagoras, not Plato, was right: that the human perspective is the measure, if not the limit, of all human knowledge. The effort to transcend humanity could only go so far before humanism would reassert its inescapability.

Part II

Faith and Reason

The Birth of Christianity

The philosophical background of Christianity is not only the ancient Hebrews but, less directly, the philosophies of Greece and the Middle East. Like Buddhism and Confucianism, Christianity developed around a single individual, Jesus, the "Christ," who lived from approximately 5 B.C.E. to 30 C.E. in Palestine, which was then part of the Roman Empire. But unlike the Buddha and Confucius, Jesus was more than human, even more than divine. He was God.

Jesus appeared in Jerusalem as the *Messiah*. (The word *Messiah* also means "the anointed," as does the Greek word *Christ*.) He was crucified by the Roman rulers, and his death marked one of the great ruptures of Western thinking. Philosophically, Jesus stressed God's mercy and *forgiveness* rather than God's wrath, in contrast to the portrayal of an often harsh and punitive God in the Hebrew Bible. He did not call into question God's sometimes unpredictable justice, however, and he was particularly critical of those who invoked God's justice because they considered themselves especially worthy. He insisted, instead, "No one goes to God who does not go through me."

Jesus' teachings encompassed themes that were already central to Jewish thought—for example, love and the importance of helping the unfortunate. But he also taught the by-no-means-orthodox thesis that the Jewish law could be summarized in terms of loving God with one's whole heart and loving one's neighbor as oneself. This emphasis on love is stressed by Christians as a new law, a *law of love*. Jesus criticized those who made great shows of their holiness but who failed to show compassion, a theme once again borrowed from the Hebrew prophets.

Like the Jews, the Christians held that there is one God, who created the world out of nothing. But while embracing monotheism, Christians nevertheless contended that the one God is three persons, the *Holy Trinity*. One of these persons, the Father, is characterized much as the Jewish God is characterized, with emphasis placed on his power and his role in creation. The second, the Son, is God as manifest in the person of Jesus Christ, God incarnate in human flesh. The third is the *Holy Spirit*, often described as the immanence of God as he dwells among human beings. The mystery of the God-man, who chose to be born and to die in time, is known as the *Incarnation*. This idea was particularly shocking after centuries of Jewish emphasis on God's distinctness from human beings. So, too, the idea that God is in any sense *immanent*, within and among humanity, was a sharp departure from the strictly *transcendent* conception of God of the Hebrews (although the idea of immanence was already long-standing in many of the philosophies of Asia).

Christianity, like Judaism and Zoroastrianism, was particularly concerned with the problem of evil, the prevalence of suffering in a world watched over by a caring (now loving) God. Christians, like Jews, explain the prevalence of evil in terms of human sinfulness. Christians thus embrace Genesis and the story of Adam and Eve and their Fall as an account of how suffering came into the human world. The unique Christian contribution to this theory of suffering is the contention that humanity remained in a "fallen" position until Jesus Christ was crucified, although he himself was innocent. Christ thus took upon himself the guilt of humanity and the suffering necessary to expiate this guilt. It is a profound and, in the context of the long Jewish tradition of guilt and self-blame, an extremely relieving idea. It is also, in terms of any ordinary notions of justice or redemption, an extremely difficult notion.

According to the Christian Gospels, Jesus' sacrifice opens the way to salvation, now understood as eternal life in union with God. Thus, the crucifixion is seen by Christians as putting things right between God and humanity. Although belief in an *afterlife* had never been the official doctrine among the Jews, it became one of the basic tenets of Christian doctrine. Thus, the idea of individual salvation became the cornerstone of Christian philosophy. The ultimate personal question of Christian theology becomes, How is one to be saved? Meanwhile, the doctrine of the Trinity would create numerous tensions within the view that God is one.

BECAUSE JUDAISM AND then Christianity were religions that came to rely on the written word, the Hebrew Bible, and the Gospels respectively, they both faced important issues of interpretation. Jewish scholarship and Greek philosophy both raised a particularly significant perplexity concerning the role of reason in interpreting Scripture, the holy writings. Could reason provide the tools for interpretation? If a thesis surpassed rational understanding, as the God-man doctrine seemed to, should reason give way to faith, or should faith give way to reason? The history of Judaism pointed to the conclusion that faith, above all, is essential. The dialectical activity of the rabbis and the Greek philosophers, however, indicated an important role for reason.

These issues quite naturally came to a head when the Jewish religion confronted Greek philosophy in the final centuries of the millennium. *Philo* (20 B.C.E.–40 C.E.) was one of the first Jewish thinkers to draw upon Greek thought in his efforts to establish the proper approach for interpreting Scripture. Living in Alexandria, the center of Hellenistic culture, Philo was personally sensitive to the conflicts between the two traditions he inherited. As a Jew, he was committed to monotheism and resistant to assimilation. On the other hand, the culture and the philosophical tradition in which he had been educated were distinctively Greek. This question of whether to maintain one's Jewish identity or assimilate into the dominant culture has fostered one of the longest debates in Jewish history, and the issue goes right to the heart of the question of self-identity.

But this question, in turn, spurred Philo's interest in synthesizing Jewish thought in Greek terms and harmonizing it with reasoned argumentation. Philo reinterpreted Biblical tales as mythic statements about the nature of the human condition and humanity's relationship to the divine. Philo went on to suggest that the Greek philosophers had been inspired by the same God who had revealed himself through Scripture. Philo underplayed tales of the miraculous and those aspects of Scripture that mark off the Jews as the uniquely "chosen" people. Like the Stoics, Philo conceived of God as pervading the world such that an inner divine spark was evident within every human being. Although God himself is transcendent, he is nevertheless related to the material world through *logos* (the world's underlying structure). Plato's Socrates had described the dazzling insight provided by even a glimpse of the Forms, and many Jews similarly believed that one should aim at a mystical vision of God. It is easy to see how these two ideas fit together and how Plato's Good could later become the Christian God. Nevertheless, reasoning could only take humanity so far. God's essence remained beyond the reach of the human mind. Reason, in other words, had to be supplemented by faith.

PHILO'S PHILOSOPHY WAS extremely well suited to early Christianity. As Christianity opened its doors and began to actively recruit new members, Philo's Hellenistic interpretation of the Hebrew God made the new religion easily accessible to the Greeks ("gentiles"). But this abstract Platonic interpretation was not enough. What was also needed was an attractive presentation of the significance of Christianity for personal salvation and an intelligible interpretation of the God-man idea. These were provided in the earliest days of Christianity by *(Saint) Paul* (c. 10–65 C.E.).

Like Philo, Paul was a Hellenized Jew. Although he was an enthusiastic persecutor of Christians in his early adulthood, he became an equally ardent defender of the faith after his conversion. Paul claimed that he was knocked off his horse on the road to Damascus, found himself temporarily blinded, and heard a voice ask, "Why do you persecute me?" Thus "seeing the light," Paul converted to Christianity. And with his conversion, he came to encourage a universalist view of Christianity, insisting that the new religion should not differentiate between Jews and Greeks. There were no special provisions for the "chosen people." It was Paul who interpreted Jesus as the Son of God and who introduced the notion of the Holy Spirit as imparting grace into the hearts of the Christian community. Grace is the blessing of God and the key to salvation. It was Paul who interpreted Jesus' crucifixion as an *atonement* for all human sins. God will decide who is to be saved, he said, and he anticipated that the Second Coming of Christ would be relatively soon, as did most of his early Christian followers.

Neoplatonism, Augustine, and the Inner Life of Spirit

Greek thought had considerable influence on Christian thought, mediated by a number of philosophies called *Neoplatonism*, based on

Plato's thought. (In addition to its impact on Christianity, Neoplatonism also had significant impact on Islamic thought, as we shall see.) The most influential of the Neoplatonist thinkers was *Plotinus* (ca. 205–269 C.E.). Plotinus emphasized the religious currents in Plato's thought, facilitating the conflation of Platonic metaphysics with Christian theology. For example, he interpreted the Platonic form of the Good as the Supreme Mind, inviting further interpretation of the Good as the Christian God. As an intelligence, this Supreme Mind was engaged in contemplation of itself, and Creation emerged as a kind of overflow from its thinking. Creation, in other words, emanated, or issued from, God's thinking. Plotinus's theory is often described as a theory of *emanations*.

In contrast to Plato, who denigrated the material world as a lesser reality (comparing it to the shadows in a cave), Plotinus saw the material world as itself spiritual, the thought of a fully spiritual mind. Plotinus did, however, believe that the world's emanations comprised a hierarchy, with one order of being emerging from another. Spirit, the highest form of being, emerges directly from the Divine Mind. Spirit illuminates Plato's Forms, the objects of the Divine Mind's contemplation. Soul proceeds from Spirit and guides life in the world by reaching beyond itself, ensouling matter. Matter is merely the lowest of the emanations.

In the first centuries of Christianity, this theory had tremendous appeal because it satisfied both philosophical and religious demands. Plato had divided the divine realm from the material realm without providing much of an account of their relationship. The theory of emanations tries to explain this. But Plotinus's spiritual outlook is also appealing because it does not try to remove the "mystery" from the Platonic account of the world, and it conveys a remarkably positive spiritual message. The human soul is already in some sense divine, and even the material world of everyday life is spiritual. Moreover, there is no evil in the world and therefore no "problem" of evil. What we encounter is an absence of good, which can, through human devotion, be corrected.

ST. AUGUSTINE (354–430 C.E.) elaborated Plotinus's message that evil was only the absence of good. After a youthful period of wanton sensuality, Augustine began seeking a solution to the problem of evil. The first solution that attracted him was that of the Manicheans, who like Zoroaster believed that the world was a manifestation of a great battle between good and evil. Augustine soon became disillusioned with this and pursued Neoplatonism through the works of Plato and Plotinus. After he converted to Christianity at the age of thirty-three, he fully devoted himself to the task of philosophically integrating Christian doctrine with Platonic and Neoplatonic philosophy. From Plotinus, Augustine accepted the view that true reality is spiritual and all being comes from God. He read Plotinus's articulation of the levels of emanation in terms of the Christian doctrine of the Trinity. From Plato, he came to accept the view that a life of contemplation was the only way to knowledge and happiness. As a Christian, he embraced the view that the proper guide to revelation was Scripture.

In creating the world, God had constructed human beings and all other creatures perfectly, giving them natures that were designed for pursuing their natural and (in the case of human beings) supernatural ends. According to Augustine, his Greek philosophical predecessors had described the natural purposes of human beings quite aptly, but they had been deluded or unclear about their supernatural destinies, mystical union with God in a state of blessedness. This in turn suggested a series of solutions to the problem of evil (which had not, Augustine thought, been dissolved by Plotinus). While natural disasters that caused suffering might suggest otherwise, Augustine insisted that we simply could not see their ultimate significance in the entire plan that God had for his Creation. If we could conceive of God's plan, we would see that his Creation was entirely good (as in Plotinus). But an essential part of this divine plan was to allow human beings an intimate share in God's own nature, by granting them the great blessing of *free will*.

Unlike other aspects of Creation, which followed God's plan without fail, human beings, Augustine said, were allowed to determine their own actions. The culminating perfection of God's Creation was that God allowed human beings to freely choose to believe in him and to join with him in actualizing his plan. But because human beings have free choice, God cannot be said to have caused them to sin. The possibility of sin is a necessary feature of free will. Far from causing human beings to sin, God gave human beings the ability to overcome sin and offers them *grace* as well as divine guidance.

Perhaps Augustine's greatest single contribution to Western philosophy was his exploration of and emphasis on one's personal, inner life. The statement "I think, therefore I am," famously attributed to

Descartes, appeared in the writings of Augustine twelve centuries earlier. It was Augustine, more than any other philosopher, who introduced and described in exquisite detail "inner" or "subjective" experience. Augustine's spiritual autobiography, *The Confessions*, remains one of the boldest and most frank investigations of the self in Western literature.

Augustine came to see the relationship between God and the human soul as the central concern of religion. Because the soul was created "in the image of God," self-knowledge had become a means of coming to know God. It is thus with Augustine that we follow one of the most dramatic turns in philosophy, the "inward" turn (though we might note that a comparable turn appeared in Buddhism many centuries before, and certainly Socrates had been on this track as well). With Augustine, the personal, inner life of the spirit starts to take center stage in Western thinking.

To Mecca: The Rise of Islam

Muhammad (c. 570–632 C.E.), a merchant in Mecca, became the central prophet and founder of Islam. (The term "Islam" derives from *salam*, meaning "peace and surrender," namely, the peace that comes from surrender to God.) When Muhammad was in his forties, he went into the mountains for a religious retreat and experienced a revelation. He was commanded to "recite" by the angel Gabriel, and the "recitations" that he uttered were divine revelation. The *Qur'an* is a transcription of these revelations. The words of the Qur'an are considered so holy that even the letters on the page are sacred. (Accordingly, there are no true translations of the Qur'an from Arabic, only "interpretations"). Islam, like Judaism and Christianity, is a religion "of the book."

Before Islam, the religions of the Arabic world involved the worship of many spirits, called *jinn*; Allah was but one of many gods worshipped in Mecca. But then Muhammad taught the worship of Allah as the only God, whom he identified as the same God worshipped by Christians and Jews. He also accepted the authenticity of both the Jewish prophets and Jesus, and so do his followers. Muslims, however, believe that Muhammad himself was the last and greatest prophet, whose mission was to restore true monotheism, proclaim God's mercy, and unify the diverse Arabic families into a single nation conjoined by a common faith.

Like the religion of the ancient Hebrews, Islam served as a potent political force. The Arabs were the "chosen people" of the Qur'an, which traces their origin (as the Hebrew's Bible traces their origin) to Abraham. Nevertheless, Islam was open to all those who worshipped the same God—to Christians and Jews as well as Arabs. Consequently, controversies ensued about the extent to which this universal appeal should be balanced against the specific conception of Islam as a religion of the Arabs. These controversies paralleled debates in early Christianity about whether that movement should be understood as a Jewish sect or a universalistic creed that embraced non-Jews on equal terms.

The appeal of Islam was its simplicity and the fact that it pervaded everyday life. The main requirement of Islam is a single affirmation: the believer must affirm, at least once during his or her life, "There is no God but God (Allah), and Muhammad is his prophet." This requirement is the first of the *Five Pillars of Islam*, the basic obligations of the believer. (The other four are: prayer, almsgiving, the observance of Ramadan as a month of fasting and a pilgrimage to Mecca once during the believer's lifetime.)

Philosophically, a powerful notion of social and economic *justice* underlies the teachings of Islam, as evidenced by the third Pillar, with its emphasis on charity. A good deal of Islamic theological speculation begins with the axiom that God is perfectly just. Justice, however, has two complementary meanings. One is compassion, exemplified by charity; the other is retribution. A person who does wrong must be punished, just as a person who does right should be rewarded. The Islamic conception of *jihad* (holy war) should be understood in terms of justice, as resistance to evil. The notion of *jihad* also extends to the inner life, and the "struggle on behalf of God" includes the believer's inner struggles in the effort to bring greater religious awareness to his or her life and society. The assurance of God's justice is the Islamic solution to the problem of evil. People are responsible for their behavior, and God is just in punishing wrongdoers because human beings have free will. Like Christians, Muslims believe that individuals have immortal souls that go to heaven or hell after death, so that crimes that are not punished and virtues that are not rewarded in life will justly be dealt with nevertheless.

The Islamic worldview is fundamentally egalitarian in both its metaphysics and its social philosophy. Unlike the Platonic and neo-Platonic traditions, which see the material world as inferior, Islam considers the material world to be both real and good. (The strong tradition of science in medieval Islam is a direct reflection of this belief in the value of the natural world.) And socially, Islam takes everyone to be equal in the eyes of God. But a doctrine of universal equality complicates the interpretation of the Qur'an. One prominent view in certain sects of Islam is that the Qur'an has several layers of meaning—the *exoteric* level, the literal meaning evident to all readers and accessible through reason and common sense, and a deeper *esoteric* level, available only to those who are properly trained and initiated. Those who accept these multiple levels of meaning believe that a proper understanding of the Qur'an must ultimately depend on the authority of well-trained and privileged individuals. (Whether or not there are such priviledged individuals is, of course, a continuing controversy in Judaism and Christianity as well.)

Altered States: Mysticism and Zen

Mysticism is a philosophy (or, perhaps, a special conception of experience) that cuts across a great many religious traditions, including all three of the great Western religions. Mysticism is the transformation of consciousness to gain access to higher orders of reality than those ordinarily experienced. The Hindu practice of yoga, for example, is a discipline in which the practitioner employs techniques for gaining control over the mind and the body with the ultimate aim of union with the Brahman. Many Buddhists, similarly, employ disciplined meditation as a means of transcending the illusory constraints of the everyday mind. Jewish and Christian mystical interpreters also insist that true insight results from gaining access to higher levels of reality. Two excellent examples are the organized esotericism of the early Christian Gnostic sects, who believed that insight depended on initiation into secret knowledge, and the Spanish mystic Teresa of Avila (1515–1582), who documented in often erotic detail her mystical experiences.

Being a mystic could be dangerous business. The most widely read Christian mystic, Meister Eckhardt (c. 1260–c. 1327), was a German Dominican who faced charges of heresy. His works were condemned by the Pope. Eckhardt's statements sounded too much like denials of orthodox doctrines; for example, he suggested that Creation was one with the Creator and co-eternal with God. Al Hallaj, an Islamic mystic, was assassinated in 922 C.E. for crying "I am God" while at the peak of a religious experience.

Jewish mysticism stresses the fact that Scripture can be understood on a number of levels, with certain higher levels of interpretation accessible only to those who are properly trained and initiated. Jewish mystics find "inner teachings" within Scripture, and they also make use of the *kabbalah*, which comprises the tradition of mystical texts that began to appear during the Middle Ages. (The term *kabbalah* literally means "tradition.") Kabbalistic thought developed an interpretation of the Torah in terms of a theory of ten emanations (called *sefiroth*). God is the ultimate source of all that exists, but nothing can be said about God as such.

Most mystical traditions stand well within the scope of orthodoxy, and some (such as the Jewish Hassidic community) are quite conservative religiously. Nevertheless, the fact that mysticism depends on individual efforts and experiences creates a philosophical problem—and sometimes a practical one—for the authority of organized religion.

Sufism, a prominent mystical tradition within Islam, refuses to believe that access to the esoteric levels is restricted to an elite group of holy men and their disciples. Sufis believe that *divine grace* renders the esoteric levels of meaning available to anyone who is devoted to Sufi mystical practice. Sufis cultivate various stages of self-perfection in the quest to reach the ideal condition of complete absorption in God. Ultimately, the believer achieves *gnosis*, the elimination of the ego, an experience of ecstasy in which the believer becomes one with God and knows the full truth: that God created the world from love, as an overflow of his own being.

AROUND THE END of the millenium, at the other end of the planet, Buddhism spread from China to Japan. *Zen* synthesized traditional Japanese religion and Buddhism and coincided with the emergence of the samurai warrior class. The relative simplicity of Zen appealed to the samurais in much the same way that the relative simplicity of Islam appealed to the warriors of Arabia. Earlier forms of Buddhism had emphasized scholarship, good works, and ascetic practices. Zen de-emphasized these and taught that anyone could attain enlightenment (*satori* in Japanese). What was necessary was to break down usual patterns of everyday, logical thinking. Zen urged meditation as a means to this end. One traditional technique is the use of a koan, a conundrum such as "What is the sound of one hand clapping?" Our usual habits of thought are so little equipped to deal with such a question that they are subverted by the process of meditating on it.

A sense of the innovation that Zen represented can be gleaned by comparing its simplicity and universality with the aestheticism and elitism evident in the writings of *Sei Shonagon* (b. 966) and Lady Murasaki Shikibu (978–1015) a century or so earlier in Japan. Shonagon's diary, or "pillow book," is one of the most significant works in Japanese literature, and Murasaki's *Tale of Genji* is widely recognized as the world's first novel. During the last decade of the tenth century C.E., both were ladies-in-waiting in the imperial court. While not by any means systematic works of philosophy, the *Pillow Book* and *Genji* convey a philosophical vision that values beauty and aesthetic contemplation. Both reflect the political elitism of the era. (One might also see in both works a proto-feminist attitude toward men, to whom the authors clearly felt themselves equal.)

Perhaps the greatest of the early Zen Buddhists was *Dōgen* (1200–1253), who insisted on Zen as a philosophical discipline. Convinced that the body and mind are a unity, Dōgen promoted a specific posture for meditation called *zazen* (literally, seated meditation). The purpose of this practice is to enter a state of mind that is pre-reflective, or "without thinking," as Dōgen describes it. By emptying one's mind of all its usual categorizations and conceptualizations, one becomes receptive to the Buddhist insight that nothing is what it is "in itself." Things are what they are only because of their relationships to everything else. When one gains this insight, according to Dōgen, one sees the "nothingness" of everything. All that exists is "the Buddha-nature," and everything within this nature shares in the Buddha's "enlightened" condition.

Reason and Faith: The Peripatetic Tradition

If there was a single dispute that captured the core of philosophy between the first and second millennia, it was the debate over faith and reason and their role in religion. Within Islam, some theologians defended the centrality of *reason* in interpreting the Qur'an, but the role of reason would be problematic in Islam for reasons similar to those invoked in Jewish and Christian theology. Some Muslims questioned the appropriateness of using human reason in attempting to understand Allah, who surpasses our human faculties, while others considered reason to be a gift from God and thus perfectly appropriate in religion. Such debates were particularly prevalent in the tradition of thinkers known as Peripatetics (because of their admiration for Aristotle, who "walked around" as he lectured), a tradition whose influence extended beyond Islam to the rest of the West.

As the Arabs invaded the Persian and Byzantine empires, they imposed their language and religion on the peoples they conquered. The influence, however, worked in both directions. After the Arabs encountered Greek, Jewish, and Christian traditions of philosophical discourse, they set about developing a similar tradition on their own. Islam became centered in Baghdad, and Arabic became the reigning scholarly language. During the period from approximately 750 to 900 C.E., many Greek works were translated into Arabic, including works by Plato, Aristotle, and Plotinus. Drawing on these, Arabic scholars developed their own philosophical vocabulary. Certain terms were directly transposed from the Greek, including *falsafah*, a transposition of the Greek *philosophia*.

Using Aristotle, Arabic and Persian philosophers tried to systematize all knowledge. The Peripatetics were strongly influenced by Plotinus, with the result that their interpretations of Aristotle were often elaborated in terms of "emanations." The Persian philosopher *al-Kindi* (ca. 800–866), for example, followed Aristotle but accepted Plotinus's notion that all of creation consisted of a series of emanations from the Divine Unity. So, too, *Ibn Sina* (or "Avicenna," 980–1037) contended that emanations from God's intellect formed a hierarchy, with our world on the lowest level. He presented God as transcendent and distant from the world of everyday human concerns, but nevertheless held that all of God's creatures were attached to God by love.

Ibn Rushd (or "Averroës," 1126–1198) attacked the view that Creation emanated from the Divine and insisted that God was not distant but actively involved in the world and wholly knowledgeable about his creatures. By rejecting the Neoplatonic scheme, Ibn Rushd gave a reading of Aristotle that was more naturalistic than that of his Peripatetic predecessors. He argued that reason was compatible with revelation, although he admitted that truth exists in various degrees. The Qur'an offered truth to all kinds of individuals, but it provided truth to different temperaments in different ways. The literal word might be sufficient for ordinary individuals, but educated people also required persuasive argument. Thus the important role of reason.

Because Arabic was the medieval language of scholarship, even some scholars outside the Islamic tradition wrote their philosophical works in

Arabic. Foremost of them was *Moses Maimonides* (1135–1204), a Spanish-born Jew who settled in Egypt. One of Maimonides' great accomplishments was to organize and systematize the Mishnah, the rabbinical reflections on the Hebrew Scripture that had developed over the centuries. Like most of his era's Arab and Persian philosophers, Maimonides took Aristotle's philosophy as his foundation. Aristotle's influence is evident in his most famous work, *Guide to the Perplexed*, in which Maimonides attempted to reconcile religion with reason. He contended that philosophy should be subordinate to revelation, but that reason could, nevertheless, be used to defend certain truths made known through revelation. In particular, Maimonides contended that knowledge of science should not lead to the abandonment of religion, an important point in the years to come and one widely accepted by the Islamic scholars.

Thinking God: Scholasticism

Scholasticism marked the high point of theology in medieval Christian thought between approximately 1050 and 1350. It centered around a method of philosophical speculation that was grounded in Aristotle. The Scholastics shared a commitment to the fundamental premises of the Catholic faith and a belief that human reason could be utilized to extend the truths learned in revelation. They were influenced in their view of reason by Augustine's belief that the same God who was revealed through Scripture had given human beings the faculty of reason, which enabled them to come to know the truth. The Scholastics were heavily influenced by the Peripatetics.

The most noteworthy figure of the early Scholastic period was *Saint Anselm* (ca. 1033–1109). Anselm acknowledged Augustine as a source, although he did not share Augustine's enthusiasm for the Platonic Forms or Neoplatonic emanations. Anselm's philosophical enterprise was to explore the mysteries of faith. His motto was "Faith seeking to understand." Accordingly, Anselm approached his subject matter with great feeling as well as intelligence. He was convinced that at least some truths known by revelation could also be demonstrated by logically rigorous argumentation. Anselm's most famous argument was (what Kant later called) the *ontological proof* for the existence of God, perhaps influenced by Ibn Sina. An ontological proof proceeds by showing that the very concept of something entails its existence. Anselm did not for a moment intend his proof as a means of persuading nonbelievers; he only insisted that it made the nature of God clearer to those who already had faith.

In his ontological proof, Anselm argued that the very definition of God implies God's existence. God, according to Anselm, is "that than which none greater can be conceived." Even those who do not believe in God understand that this is what is meant by "God." God is by definition the most perfect being and so no greater being can be conceived. What follows from this is that God, so understood, must exist, for if God were a mere possibility, a glorious idea without a referent, one could conceive of a still more perfect being—namely, one that shared all the perfections of the idea but also existed. Once one accepts the conception of God as the most perfect conceivable being, one is logically committed to the existence of God as well.

Peter Abelard (1079-1142) was the outstanding logician of the Scholastic period. To history, Abelard is best known as the beloved of his student Héloise. The letters exchanged between them constitute one of the most moving collections of love correspondence in Western literature. As a philosopher, however, Abelard was primarily interested in what we now call the philosophy of language. He believed, as do many philosophers today, that most theological and philosophical confusions are the result of confusions about language, about the meanings of words.

Abelard's philosophical reputation is attached to his **doctrine of names**, or **nominalism**. He argued, first of all, that words are just names, "signifiers." (The things they indicate are their "signifieds.") But what sorts of words are names?—for not all words in fact designate entities. Abelard noted, in particular, a question that dated back to Plato and Aristotle concerning words that refer to classes (that is, open-ended groups or types of individuals, e.g., "cats"), properties (which are universal in that any number of different objects can share the same property, e.g., being red), and ideal types (e.g. "triangle"). The question, the "problem of universals," was whether such words refer in fact to real entities, namely, the essence or Platonic Form of being a cat, the color red, or the perfect triangle.

Some logicians, called *realists*, insisted that there were such peculiar entities. Others, called *conceptualists*, insisted that universals exist only in the mind. Abelard, by contrast, takes the radical view that nothing exists except individuals. He denies the existence of universals and rejects the view of those realists who claim that things have essences that make them the things that they are. There is no Platonic Form or essence of cat, only numerous cats. There is no color red, only innumerable red things. There is no Platonic Form triangle, only triangles. Words trick us into thinking in terms of universals, but universals are not real. They are only the constructions that we postulate when we use language.

Abelard applied this sharp distinction between words and realities to his interpretation of Scripture. He suggested that apparent conflicts among religious authorities were likely to be resolved by seeing that they used the same words in different ways. Abelard was the first to use the term "theology" in the modern sense, to refer to the rational investigation of the mysteries of religion. Entering into what had now become a millennium-old argument, Abelard defended the application of reason to revelation, contending that faith was only opinion if not defended by reason. Since he believed that reason provided insight into religious truth, he insisted that the ancient Greeks went admirably far in the direction of Christian teaching, even glimpsing to some extent the nature of the Trinity.

Thomas Aquinas (Thomas of Aquino, c. 1225–1274) is the culminating figure of Scholasticism. Thomas aimed to show that Christian faith was grounded in reason and that the law inherent in nature is rational. He was particularly influenced by Aristotle, whose significance he so took for granted (as did so many of his contemporaries) that he referred to him simply as "the Philosopher." Thomas was also a great synthesizer, who contended that reason and revelation each had its own realm. Reason was an appropriate instrument for learning the truth about the natural world; revelation concerned the supernatural world. The true place of the natural world could only be known by reference to the supernatural.

The distinction between the realms of reason and of revelation allowed Thomas to specify a distinct place for Aristotle's philosophy in a Christian worldview. Thomas's endorsement of Aristotelian philosophy made room within Christian thought for a relatively high regard for the natural world and human activities within it. This contrasted with the more Platonic cast of earlier Christian thought, which had emphasized the unreality of the natural world in comparison with the real and heavenly world of the Forms. But Thomas also considered the natural world to be a reflection of the law of God. In recognizing the intelligible structure of the world of everyday experience through reason, therefore, human beings gain insight into the mind of God as well. Thomas's account was a major boost for the study of science when science was still largely on the defensive.

Seeing the work of God's law throughout the natural world, Thomas claimed that reason would be led to God by contemplating nature. Thomas provided his own arguments for the existence of God in the form of *cosmological proofs*, an inference from factual existence to ultimate explanation. For example, the motion of contingent things is causally dependent on other things that move them. Believing, with Aristotle, that an infinite regress is unintelligible, Thomas was convinced that this realization would lead the mind to seek a Prime Mover. In each of his five proofs of God's existence (also called his "Five Ways"), Thomas made a similar inference, from the contingent being of things in the natural world to a necessary being who transcends them, namely God.

So, too, human morality is neither simply a matter of freedom nor the outcome of our animal natures, but depends on the particular God-given nature of human beings. Morality like nature depends on *natural law*, moral principles instilled in us and discoverable through reason. Nevertheless, despite his emphasis on rationality, Thomas insisted on the limitations of reason. Revelation is necessary, he argued, for insight into the divine realm of God in heaven.

"Rebirth" in Religion and Philosophy: Renaissance and Reformation

Until the fifteenth century or so, the Catholic church dominated the philosophy of most of Europe. Then two great convulsions challenged the authority and the religious perspective of the church. One was the *Renaissance* ("rebirth"), which spread across Europe in the late fifteenth century. The other was the *Reformation*, which began more precisely on October 31, 1517, when *Martin Luther* (1483–1546) nailed 95 "theses" to the door of the Wittenberg cathedral.

The Renaissance was above all a resurgence of humanism and the dignity of the individual, supported by a newly sophisticated and cultured urban class. It was a literary and artistic movement whose most valued products were the "humanities," those disciplines that came to be expected of every educated citizen. But Renaissance humanism was not, contrary to the accusations of polemicists both then and today, exclusively secular or Godless. In many ways, the Renaissance remained medieval and sometimes mystical, and it is important to remember that the new emphasis on the dignity of the individual was born and nourished within the embrace of Christianity and the Judeo-Christian tradition.

The Renaissance was not so much a time of "starting over," as some of its more aggressive advocates suggested, as a time of rejuvenation, enthusiasm, and experimentation. In particular, it was the rediscovery of, or at any rate a new emphasis on, the classics, the literature of the ancient Greeks and Romans. In that sense, of course, the Renaissance owed its existence to the Islamic world, which had preserved many of the texts that had been proscribed by the Church.

The Renaissance was also a sigh of relief from the horrors of history. We can understand the exhilaration that accompanied the passing of the plague (the "Black Death") which had destroyed a third of the population of Europe, and the end of the Hundred Years War between England and France, which had destroyed so many as well. Renaissance humanism can be seen as a recoil from those awful years. Feudalism had all but collapsed, and a new mercantilism and a sense of exploration dominated Europe, soon to be fed by a new "capitalist" impulse.

MOST PROTESTANTS VIEW the Reformation as a movement devoted to moral reform within Christianity. The Reformation too, was rooted in humanism (as well as in nationalism, which defined religious groups within cultural and historical parameters). Luther's most immediate philosophical concern was that perennial problem of the Western tradition, the problem of evil, of sin and redemption. Ever since Saint Paul, one of the most appealing features of Christianity had been the forgiveness of sins. It was not obvious, however, how the individual could be certain that his or her sins were forgiven. Luther was convinced that the Catholic Church had become so corrupted that it was now manipulating believers' doubts and fears by *selling* forgiveness, by way of what were called *indulgences*. The very idea of indulgences presupposed that human actions (whether the recitation of prayers or the giving of alms) could have an impact on one's salvation. In Luther's view, this idea was tantamount to the claim that one could bribe God or buy salvation.

Drawing on Augustinian philosophy, Luther emphasized the sinful nature of humanity. Human beings, he said, are inherently torn, divided between the desires of the flesh and the aspirations of the spirit. This internal war of flesh and spirit culminates in *despair*, although God offers grace which cannot be bought or earned. Luther denied that good works were either necessary or sufficient to ensure salvation. Christians had an obligation to love and serve others, but the fulfillment of that obligation was not a condition of salvation.

Part of the humanistic tradition was its emphasis on feeling in religious matters, personal faith, and Luther exemplified this aspect of humanism. He opposed Scholasticism, with its emphasis on rational argument, and he was no fan of Aristotle or Aquinas. In the fallen state of humanity, he argued, all human faculties were corrupted, including reason. Reason was too often hubristic, attempting to explain matters of faith that are beyond reason's capacity. Genuine faith requires experience, not demonstration, and this experience is available to everyone. Luther's insistence that faith alone was essential to salvation reiterated the emphasis on the "inner," so evident in Augustine. The faithful could and should trust in God's mercy and maintain an attitude of humility and repentance. Christianity was now to be located in the inner life of the spirit, not in the institution of the church or a system of theology.

UNLIKE LUTHER, THE French reformer *John Calvin* (1509–1564) emphasized the importance of an institutional church and a system of theology. The new emphasis on the "inner" gave license to some wild individual conceptions of faith, so in response to religious and philosophical anarchy, Calvin insisted on some clear basis to distinguish religious truth from heresy. Moreover, he went even further than Luther had gone in emphasizing human sinfulness. Human beings were so corrupted by original sin, he argued, that even newborn babies deserved damnation. Calvin considered humans utterly insignificant except as vehicles for illustrating God's grace in action.

Even though sinners resisted God's will, according to Calvin, they could not act apart from it. In a sense, therefore, God condoned their sinfulness. Calvin articulated this paradoxical relationship of God to sin in his doctrine of *predestination*. In accounting for why some people but not others heard the word of God, Calvin argued that God had elected and predestined those who would be saved and those who would be damned. But even that relatively small percentage of human beings who would be saved did not *deserve* salvation, being sinners. God simply chose to forgive them. His forgiveness was a gift to the elect.

Election could not be earned. People naturally wanted to know, "will I be saved?" Thus, despite the Protestant de-emphasis of human efforts and good works, many Protestants became obsessed with work. Worldly success became a sign of blessedness. Modern capitalism, it has been argued, was the fruit of this obsession.

THE REFORMATION NATURALLY prompted a reaction in the Catholic church, the Counter-Reformation. In the ongoing clash between them, Europe would experience some of its bloodiest decades. But the conflict between the Church and the Reformation should not be separated entirely from the Renaissance, which established a sophisticated level of learned debate. The religious turmoil thus produced some great philosophers, for example, the Dutchman *Desiderius Erasmus* (1469–1530), a leading biblical scholar. He is best represented by a timely satire, *In Praise of Folly*. In the midst of the Counter-Reformation and the Inquisition, Erasmus reminded us that most of what is of worth in human life is not due to wisdom or piety but to foolishness. Who would get married, have children, enter politics, fall in love, or become a philosopher if he or she actually possessed the wisdom to foresee the consequences and the implications? Quoting Sophocles with approval, Erasmus defended the highly anti-philosophical position that "the happiest life is to know nothing at all." In an era of violent religous controversies, that bit of pseudo-Socratic humility was most welcome.

The New Science and its Politics

The Renaissance emphasis on the humanities included a new respect for science, fueled by developments in technology and mathematics and in particular by the most spectacular scientific revolution. Nicolus Copernicus (1473-1543) argued that the sun, not the earth, is the center of our universe. The pursuit of scientific knowledge, which had long had a secondary relationship to the larger dogma of theology, now began its quick ascendancy, resulting in a protracted and sometimes brutal antagonism with the Church. In 1600, Giordano Bruno was burnt at the stake for heresy, and soon after, Galileo was forced to recant his Copernican view (a position not officially accepted by the Catholic church until 1992!).

It would be a mistake to exaggerate the ongoing conflict between science and religion, however. As Nature was considered to be God's "handiwork" (a conception inherited from the ancient Hebrews and defended by Thomas Aquinas), science was seen as a mode of revelation, a way of appreciating God's wonders. For the most part, the Church was perfectly happy to tolerate science so long as it did not conflict with doctrinal teaching.

In the fifteenth century, Aristotle still ruled science. Theories and hypotheses from the fourth century B.C.E. were still accepted as "common sense." After the fifteenth century, "Common sense" was no longer simply accepted. A widespread skepticism was the healthy attitude. But ironically, the emerging humanism was founded on the shocking revelation that human beings and the planet they occupied were not the center of the cosmos.

The "new science" of Copernicus and Galileo needed a philosophical defense against the dogmatism of the Church and Aristotle. It found that defender in *Francis Bacon* (1561–1626). Bacon is usually recognized as the founder of the modern scientific tradition, which means, in particular, that he broke with Aristotle and insisted that we "start over" with a purely empirical, experimental method of investigating the world. Bacon was not himself a scientist: he is not known for his theories or discoveries in the way that Copernicus, Galileo, Kepler, and Newton are known. He rather theorized *about* science, and about knowledge in general. In particular, he explicated the experimental method that would have so much influence on Galileo and the future of science. It was Bacon who formulated what has now become the textbook version of the "scientific method," which involves careful observation and the controlled, methodical experiment. The scientific method provided the call to get a fresh start on all of the questions that were supposedly answered by the ancients.

Against the dogmas of the past, Bacon attempted to justify the pursuit of knowledge "for its own sake." This should not be misunderstood, as it so often is today, as a defense of inquiry without regard for consequences. Bacon insisted on precisely the opposite, namely, that knowledge is *useful*. Indeed, he famously proclaimed, "*Knowledge is power!*" He also defended science as the ultimate dominion of humanity over nature, as promised in Genesis, and as the study of God's works, just as legitimate a source of revelation as the study of his Word.

Bacon gave an egalitarian status to science by insisting that anyone, using the right methods, could discover the truth; science was not the exclusive realm of geniuses. This would become a political claim of no small importance. But this is not to say that Bacon simply defended "common sense." One of the most powerful aspects of his philosophy was the critique of various "idols" of human nature that block or distort proper scientific inquiry. Among these are various prejudices and false notions that we are taught by our elders and do not question. There is a natural inertia or conservatism to human belief, making it difficult to give up an established, comfortable but false belief. Wishful thinking, our hopes and desires, too often eclipse careful perception and "true experience." There is also the danger that our senses are not always trustworthy, a view that Bacon shared with the ancients as well as his successor, René Descartes. Last but not least, Bacon attacked the belief in Aristotelian teleological explanations. Nature does not act as it does because objects and events have purposes, but because they obey causal laws.

THE POLITICAL ASPECT of Bacon's conception of the New Science was not lost on his friend *Thomas Hobbes* (1588–1679). Hobbes was also a trail-blazer for the New Science and a thorough-going critic of Aristotle's teleological view of the universe. He was also one of the most influential architects of modern political theory and a harsh antagonist of Aristotle's view of "natural" human sociability. As a metaphysician, not a scientist, Hobbes developed a purely materialist and mechanistic model of the world, the world as mere "matter in motion." It was, perhaps, the most depersonalized, colorless portrait of the universe since Democritus, but such radical moves always have their counterweight. Hobbes may have believed in a mechanical universe, but not a Godless one. He spent half his career (and virtually half of his most famous book, *Leviathan*) defending a materialist cosmology that did not exclude theology.

Hobbes is best-known, however, for his harsh vision of human life in the "state of nature," before the formation of society. People were selfish, he tells us in the early pages of *Leviathan,* and justice was unknown. Life was "a war of all against all" and consequently "nasty, brutish and short." In this mutually dangerous and combative context, men and women got together and formed a "social compact [contract]" for their mutual safety and advantage. They gave over some of their modest power to the "sovereign," the king who ruled over them not by divine right but by common agreement. With this agreement, humanity was further protected by the idea of justice, but justice was the product of contractual society, not its presupposition.

It is in this context, too, that we might mention a political genius who wrote almost a century before Hobbes, *Niccolò Machiavelli* (1467–1527). Machiavelli, in the midst of the chaos and corruption of Renaissance Italy, also set the stage for modern politics. The unmistakable subtext of his infamous treatise, *The Prince*, is that there is nothing moral about politics. Politics is all manipulation and strategy, not love for the people or anything so idealistic as civic responsiblity. In his *Art of War*, Machiavelli similarly treated war as a normal feature of relations between states which demanded continuous preparation and strategy, not a response to a sudden emergency in which untrained troops were hurriedly gathered for the occasion. Machiavelli and Hobbes broke with Aristotle's equation of politics and ethics, and this may be of more momentous significance than the scientific revolution initiated by Bacon. The latter may have produced new and terrifying weapons, but the former supplied the political will to use them.

Who Knows? The Role of Doubt in Descartes and Montaigne

With a burst of hope and confidence, the philosophers of the late Renaissance came to believe that genuine knowledge was both accessible and valuable for its own sake and valuable as an instrument of power. They also became skeptical in general, wary of believing whatever they had taken to be "obvious." A further and more profound paradox was this: the source of objective knowledge was to be found in one's own subjectivity, in experience. We come to know the world "outside" by looking "inside." It is not hard to see the virtue in this twin emphasis on subjectivity and objectivity. By insisting on subjectivity, the new philosophers could bypass the established authority of the church as well as divinely appointed political leaders. This emphasis on subjectivity also opened the way to a remarkable egalitarianism: establishing the truth is now up to each and every one of us. What we establish, using the proper methods of reason and experience, is true not just for ourselves but *of the world*, objectively. Nevertheless, such inward turning also produced new doubts. Are we capable of such knowledge?

Modern philosophy is born of this paradox of objectivity in subjectivity. *René Descartes* (1596–1650) is, almost everyone has agreed, the modern author of this paradox and the "father of modern philosophy."

Descartes was the philosopher who most dramatically insisted on the simultaneous turn to subjectivity and the use of logic, "the method of mathematics," to argue the way to objectivity. He was anticipated in this insistence on intellectual rigor by his countryman *Michel de Montaigne* (1533–1592), who was a moralist, not a scientist or a mathematician.

Montaigne wrote "essays," not methodological treatises. Like his predecessor Erasmus, he mused on the follies of men, not on their knowledge. He doubted whether human beings were capable of finding the truth or of recognizing it if they did find it, just as they seemed to be incapable of understanding justice or, more important, acting justly. He was an heir to the Skeptics of old, and for him the purpose of philosophy was to illuminate and inspire our spontaneous but humble natures. Thus he found the intellectual exercises of Scholasticism pointless at best, and probably damaging. Human society and philosophy were just so much vanity. And yet, the refusal to insist on knowledge can lead to another virtue, one of particular importance in troubled times—*tolerance*. Tolerance would remain in short supply throughout the modern era, cosmopolitan claims to the contrary.

The basic themes that have come to define much if not most of modern philosophy come from Descartes—his emphasis on methodology, his search for certainty, and his confidence that certainty could be found, if nowhere else, in the demonstrations of mathematics and geometry. When he was just a young boy, Descartes heard that Galileo had discovered the moons of Jupiter using a remarkable new instrument, the telescope. Such discoveries quite naturally raised all sorts of questions about the nature of knowledge, the reliability of appearances, the extent to which we are ignorant of the world, and the methods we use to examine and extend our knowledge. The New Science raised old questions about the relative dependability of reason versus the senses, and it raised new and exciting questions about how much could be known.

Descartes, like Montaigne, was deeply disturbed by the ongoing religious turmoil in Europe. Montaigne had recommended tolerance. Descartes instead recommended reason. The calm and convincing demonstrations of reason offered a welcome alternative to the belligerent and bloody religious disputes that were ripping nations apart. Descartes's most important thesis was his insistence on our ability to think for ourselves. Descartes's philosophy, accordingly, began with the demand that each of us establish for ourselves the truth of what we believe. To this end, he invented a radical method, "the method of doubt," in which he considered all of his beliefs suspicious until they could be proven to be justified.

Descartes's seductively charming approach to these questions is provided in his most popular work, (still the standard introduction to philosophy for millions of students) his *Meditations on First Philosophy* (1641). Descartes's style was borrowed from Montaigne, and it imitated an intimate, amiable personal conversation. Descartes invited us into his study, as Montaigne had invited us into his private thoughts. Yet if the style is borrowed from Montaigne, Descartes had the very opposite intent and came to a dramatically different conclusion. Montaigne intended for us to examine ourselves, using him as a mirror, to appreciate our own ignorance and to be humble and human about it. Descartes insisted that we push our doubts to their extremes, to the point of absurdity, where they will rebound and give us indubitable truth. Montaigne took us by the hand and shared his reflections. Descartes subjected us to the rigors of scholastic disputation, taking great pains to examine and defend his every move along the way. Montaigne emerged a skeptic. Descartes declared his victory over skepticism. He was not, he concluded, mistaken at all. Indeed, he never even really doubted.

Suppose, Descartes slyly suggested, there were an "evil genius," "supremely powerful and supremely intelligent, who purposely always deceives me." Suppose, for example, Descartes is mistaken in his belief that he is awake and not dreaming, that he has a body, that there is an "external world," that there is a God. How could he ever sort out what he knows from what he merely believes, what is true from what is false? Descartes's argument utilizes the mathematical method, in which every principle must be derived or "deduced" from prior principles that have already been established on the basis of other principles. Ultimately, all principles must be derived from a set of premises that are so obviously true that they are "self-evident." One such premise is Descartes's famous claim "I think, therefore I am."

This claim may look like an argument (because of the "therefore"), but it is really a revelation, the self-confirming realization that I cannot be fooled about the fact of my own existence. Once Descartes has his premise, he goes on to prove God's existence, in the mode of the Scholastics. ("It is impossible that the idea of God which is in us should not have God himself as its cause.") God's existence, in turn, can be used to establish the existence of the external world. If he can be certain of the existence of God, who is no deceiver,

Descartes can therefore be confident that whatever he conceives "clearly and distinctly" must be true. The evil genius is defeated.

A number of objections can be raised against these arguments, and one might question whether Descartes indeed doubted as vigorously and as thoroughly as he originally claimed. Nevertheless, Descartes established the basis for philosophical investigation: the demand for certainty and immunity from doubt. What is so tremendously new and important about Descartes, however, is not so much his insistence on certainty as his emphasis on subjectivity, on one's own thoughts and experience as primary. The authority of philosophy is now to be found not in the sages or the Scriptures but in the individual mind of the philosopher.

One of the by-products of Descartes's philosophy was a new emphasis on the Platonic and Christian distinction between mind and body (a distinction virtually absent in Aristotle). Descartes argues that a person is a coupling of two different substances, mental and physical, but since a substance is defined as that which is completely self-contained, the question of how mind and body interact is perplexing. The thesis that the mind and the body are separate substances has come to be known by the name "Cartesian dualism," and it continues to trouble philosophers and scientists to this day.

We should not suppose, however, that Descartes made some sort of stupid mistake, arbitrarily marking off the mind from the body as different "substances" and then finding himself unclear about how to get them together again. The dualism of mind and body was the product of many centuries of intellectual development, the progress of science, and the new-found respect for individual autonomy. Distinguishing the mind and the body provided a realm for science, concerned with the physical world, to proceed unhampered by religion or by moral concerns associated with the peculiarities of the human mind, human freedom, the human ability to "transcend" physical reality, and so on. The distinction also provided a realm for religion and human freedom that would not be threatened by science. Getting the mind and body together was not nearly so important as keeping them safely apart.

Why Do Things Happen? Spinoza, Leibniz, and Newton

Much of modern philosophy has become defined by Descartes's arguments in metaphysics and epistemology, however narrow these may be even in terms of Descartes's own interests and concerns. Behind Descartes's celebration of reason, however, lay the political and religious turmoil of his times as well as the new emphasis on science. Other philosophers followed Descartes into the realm of imaginative metaphysics, but they, too, had other concerns besides the metaphyisical nature of the world. The Dutchman *Baruch Spinoza* (1632–1677) and the German *Gottfried Wilhelm von Leibniz* (1646–1716) played off Descartes's Aristotelian notion of substance, but they were basically concerned with the meaning of life and our role in the world.

Spinoza was a Jewish free-thinker whose skepticism did not appeal to his orthodox brethren. He was excommunicated and, in effect, exiled from his community. He spent most of his unhappy life in seclusion, earning a meager living as a lens-grinder. (His death resulted from inhaling the glass dust.) Spinoza's main work is called *Ethics*, a title that has often confused readers who have opened the book expecting a philosophy of life and found instead a tangle of barbed prose dressed up like an extended geometrical treatise, complete with axioms, theorems, corollaries, and proofs.

Appearances, however, can be deceiving. Descartes introduced his logical demonstrations in the cozy context of a meditation, inviting the reader into his study and his thoughts, but Descartes's philosophy is anything but intimate and personally revealing. Spinoza, on the other hand, disguises his personal anguish and his proposed philosophical solution in the most formal and formidable deductive style. The book is, in keeping with its title, a heartfelt proposal for a better way to live, a solution to loneliness and isolation, an answer to the suffering and frustration of life. It is, in historical perspective, another in a long line of Stoic texts, very much in the tradition of Chryssipus, Epictetus, and Marcus Aurelius.

To be sure, Spinoza was attempting to carry out the Cartesian method in his use of the geometrical method, and the first part of the *Ethics* is an attempt to establish the singular conclusion that there is and can be but one substance with infinitely many attributes. According to Spinoza, since substances are by their very nature completely self-contained, there can be one and only one substance. That substance is God. God is therefore one with the universe, and the distinction between Creator and creation, "God or Nature," is illusory. (This position, that God and the universe are one and the same, is called "*pantheism*").

All individuals, including ourselves, are in fact modifications of the One Substance. There are infinitely many attributes of a substance, among them what we know as mind and body. (In a purely technical sense, this solves the troublesome mind-body problem, since mind and body are no longer different substances but just different aspects of one and the same substance.) Spinoza's claims about substance, however, have far more important implications that cannot be understood in terms of metaphysical technicalities alone.

In Spinoza's vision, there is no ultimate distinction between different individuals. We are all part of the same single substance, which is also God. This means that our sense of isolation from and opposition to one another is an illusion, and it also means that our sense of distance from God is mistaken. This edifying vision would become a powerful picture by the turn of the nineteenth century, when Christian philosophers would also try to overcome what they called "alienation" between people and peoples and the alienating concept of a transcendent God, a God "beyond" us. (Mystics, dating back to the earliest days of philosophy, often claimed such a vision for themselves.) Furthermore, since the One Substance has always existed and will always exist, our own immortality is assured.

Spinoza also defended the thesis generally known as *determinism*. Determinism is the claim that, from a given cause, the effect necessarily follows. Spinoza's determinism was not particularly concerned with science but rather with what we would probably consider more akin to *fate*. In Spinoza's view, whatever happens to us happens necessarily. Given that the universe is God, we can therefore be confident that whatever happens to us happens *for a reason*.

Determinism set the stage for Spinoza's ethical prescription. He recommended seeing ourselves as one with God and other people and seeing our lives as determined by necessity. Like the early Stoics, however, Spinoza argued that this satisfying vision of ourselves is easily distorted and disrupted by our emotions, which are "confused ideas." The early Stoics taught that the emotions were faulty judgments, based on a flawed understanding of ourselves and the world. We want what we cannot have, or we want what we already have (but do not know we have). So too, Spinoza's vision teaches us that it is pointless to want that which we are not determined to have, and that much of what we want—union with other people, oneness with God—we already have. What we need is control of our emotions, and the proper philosophical attitude for achieving this is acceptance or "resignation."

Unlike the ancient Stoics, however, Spinoza did not reject the emotions in general. Quite to the contrary, he assures us that the emotion that comes with an attitude of acceptance is *bliss*, a far preferable emotion than any other. The ultimate feeling of happiness lies not in illusory power or resistance but in this philosophical vision, which Spinoza also calls the intellectual love of God.

ACCORDING TO LEIBNIZ, the same premise—that substances are by their very nature completely self-contained—leads to the conclusion that the world consists of innumerable simple substances. These simple substances are called *monads*, each of which is self-contained and independent of all of the others. God, in this view, is the super-monad, the Creator of all of the others. Every monad is like a little self or psyche. It perceives the world—including what would seem to be interactions with other monads—from its own peculiar perspective. No monad, however, actually interacts with any other. Indeed, Leibniz insists that monads must be "windowless." A monad's "perceptions" are not perceptions in the usual sense but, rather, internal states that correspond to the internal states of all of the other monads in a "pre-established harmony," established by God.

Leibniz was also worried about life and how to live, but in contrast to Spinoza's lonely life he was an intellectual socialite. Leibniz knew everyone—the princes of Europe, all the great geniuses. (He even met Spinoza.) He discovered the calculus (which was independently discovered by Newton). He was a scientist, a lawyer, a historian, a statesman, an academic, a logician, a linguist, and a theologian. He wrote the most knowledgable book of his time on China. Leibniz was involved in philosophical discussion and correspondence throughout his life, but whether out of prudence or busy-ness, he published very little. Leibniz has mainly been considered a logician and a metaphysician, but his more moving work concerns his optimistic outlook on the world, an outlook that must be viewed in the context of the horrible wars and religious disputes that racked Europe in the seventeenth century.

Leibniz famously suggested the development of a universal language, a universal logic in which all problems could be resolved by bloodless, rational calculation. He defended as the basic principle of his philosophy what he called the "Principle of Sufficient Reason," which, as for Spinoza, gave him reason to assert that nothing happens without a reason. Since all reasons are God's reasons and God determines the universe (by creating the monads and their perceptions), we can feel confident that these reasons are *good* reasons—in fact, the very best reasons. This is one of Leibniz's best-known theses, but perhaps it is best known because it was brutally ridiculed by Voltaire in *Candide*. The thesis is that, given God's infinity of choices between different possible worlds, God would only choose the best of them, *the best of all possible worlds*.

Leibniz's logic may be debatable, but his vision is unassailably edifying. In times of turmoil, it is always a relief to believe that there is some reason behind whatever happens. Here is another classic answer to the ancient problem of evil. What we see as evil is due only to our limited vision, our failure to understand the sum total of the possibilities. If, at the end of our own particularly cynical century, it is hard for us to appreciate Leibniz's hopeful belief, we should nevertheless appreciate its power for those who have believed it.

No account of early modern philosophy would be adequate if it did not include the greatest physicist of the time, Sir *Isaac Newton* (1642–1727). Newton's physics is beyond the scope of this book, and so is the theology with which he occupied himself for the last several decades of his life. But Newton's impact on science, and his example to the world, was so much a part of the eighteenth century that no account of philosophy is possible without appreciation of his importance. He demonstrated the possibility of understanding the world in terms of a few simple, elegant principles. Furthermore, the tension that so troubled Newton, that between his material and mechanical physical theory of the world and his pious, spiritual Christianity, was a tension that was starting to preoccupy all of Europe.

Until the late seventeenth century, science had been an occasional annoyance to the religious authorities, but there was little sense of its ever constituting an overwhelming threat to religion. The threats to religion had come from within, as one religious faction battled another over some small point of theology (and, often, over some significant piece of land or political advantage). By the end of the century, however, science had come into its own, and it was no longer the source of mere annoyance and contradiction. The scientific worldview stood head-to-head against the established religious worldview, no longer David against Goliath. In many sensitive, inquisitive personalities, the apparent conflict between science and religion was becoming unbearable. Newton was one of those personalities.

The Search for Universals: Enlightenment

With the rise of science and its emerging victory over the authority of the Church, Europe found a new faith: faith in reason. The so-called *Enlightenment* emerged first in England, following fast on the scientific achievements of Isaac Newton and the swift and relatively bloodless political changes of the "Glorious Revolution" at the very end of the seventeenth century. It then moved into France, carried by young intellectuals like Voltaire who had visited England, and it culminated in the French Revolution of 1789. Then it spread South and East to Spain, Italy, and Germany, where it ran into considerable opposition from the Church in Rome and more traditional ways of thinking. Nevertheless, it is instructive to see the Enlightenment as a continuation of the "rebirth" begun in the Renaissance, a reaffirmation of humanism coupled with a new confidence in human reason.

The Enlightenment as such was not anti-religious; some of its most prominent participants were religious men (and women). But, following Descartes and the new science, the Enlightenment philosophers put great trust in their own ability to reason, their own experience, and their own intellectual autonomy, and this was bound to result in some opposition to the Church and its more authoritarian teachings (which the enlightenment philosophers called "superstitions"). In place of the sectarian battles that had bloodied the past several centuries, the Enlightenment philosophers insisted on being "cosmopolitan"—being citizens of the world, ignoring national boundaries, rejecting sectarian affiliation. Their truths would be universal truths, not to be imposed on others but to be discovered independently by them.

Quite a few of the French philosophers, in particular, were atheists, materialists who saw no place in the rational order of things for an authoritarian God. What all of the Enlightenment philosophers did agree on and believe in, however, was reason. Through reason, they believed, they would not only tap the basic secrets of nature through science, but they would establish a living paradise on earth, a society in which there would be no more misery, no more injustice. Thus, Condorcet, an Enlightenment enthusiast awaiting execution during the French Revolution, could write, "How consoling for the philosopher who laments the errors, the crimes, the injustices which still pollute the earth and of which he is often the victim, is this view of the human race, emancipated from its shackles and advancing with a firm and sure step along the path of truth, virtue and happiness!"

"Show Me!" Locke, Hume, and Empiricism

In England, *John Locke* (1632–1704) reacted critically to Descartes's confidence in reason. He suggested that, rather than abstract reason and speculation, we should place our confidence in experience, in our ability to learn and know about the world through our senses. With Locke, the enduring tradition of British *empiricism* began, jettisoning the long-standing suspicion of the senses that had persisted in the West since before Plato. Locke suggested that "all knowledge comes from the senses," and in this he was soon followed by the Irish Bishop George Berkeley and the Scottish philosopher David Hume.

As opposed to Descartes, Spinoza, and Leibniz, those "rationalists" who assumed a rather rich and complex structure of the mind, Locke assumed that the mind was a "blank tablet," to be written on by experience throughout one's life. The rationalists argued for a fair number of inborn or "innate" ideas, e.g., ideas about substance, about God. By contrast, Locke suggested that the mind is more like an empty closet, illuminated only by the light that enters from the outside.

Locke compromised his empiricism, however, in at least two critical ways. First, he yielded to the metaphysicians whom he attacked in accepting the idea that we find it necessary to talk about things-in-themselves, apart from our experience of them. One might think that Locke, according to his own method, should have concluded that all that we can ever know are the sensible properties or "qualities" of things. But this would leave us with a problem: it would seem that we do not know things at all, only clusters of properties. Locke concludes that we *infer* the existence of the thing-itself because we cannot imagine the notion of properties existing without their being properties of something. This sounds suspiciously like an innate idea, an assumption not based on experience.

Locke made a second compromise in his empiricism when he distinguished between two different kinds of properties or qualities, those we perceive as inherent in an object itself, such as its shape or mass, and those we perceive *in ourselves*, that is, in the effects that a thing has on us. An example of the latter would be color. These "secondary" qualities (as opposed to the primary qualities of shape and mass) are "in us" rather than "out there" in the world. Taking Locke's arguments seriously, however, one might conclude that everything that we experience, is in the mind, in us. There is neither a need nor a justification for talking about the world "out there."

Bishop *George Berkeley* (1632–1704) drew precisely this uncomfortable conclusion from Locke's own insistence on a purely empirical method. Berkeley was quite happy to suppose that there was no substantial world apart from the world in our minds. The world was indeed composed of ideas—a position subsequently known as *idealism*. As an authority of the Church, Berkeley saw in this view a way of placing God at the core of his philosophy. "To be is to be perceived," he insisted, but everything that exists is perceived not only by us but by God. We might also note how closely in spirit, if not in method, Berkeley's vision resembles the "monadology" of Leibniz.

David Hume (1632–1704) brought the odd consequences of empiricism fully into the open. Hume's philosophy was a thorough-going *skepticism*, the likes of which had not been seen since the ancients. Hume was one of the most brilliant of the Enlightenment enthusiasts, but he also recognized that reason—understood both as scientific method and as rationality more broadly conceived—had overstepped its limits. There is much, he saw, that reason cannot do, assurances it cannot deliver, proofs it cannot produce. Hume's skepticism was, paradoxically, the clearest example of solid, self-scrutinizing Enlightenment thinking. His conclusion was that even the best thinking cannot do what the Enlightenment thinkers thought it could do.

Hume's skepticism was based on a number of doctrines that had emerged from the debate about knowledge that had now gone on since Bacon and Descartes. Hume was an avowed empiricist. All knowledge, he repeated, must come from experience. He also accepted the distinction between experience and the world to which it refers. But, then, can our belief in the "external" world be established by way of experience? No, nor can our belief in the "external" world be established by way of deduction without simply begging the question.

Hume concluded that the most basic beliefs, upon which all of our knowledge is founded, cannot be established by reason. Similarly, in the realm of morals, Hume applied his skeptical eye and concludes that "it is not against reason that I should prefer the destruction of half the world to the pricking of my little finger." Reason cannot motivate us to be moral. Nevertheless, our emotions can and do. Each of us is born with a natural capacity for *sympathy* and a natural concern for *utility* (about as nuts-and-bolts a practical notion as philosophers ever employ) with which we construct, among other things, our ideas about justice and society.

Hume tended to *naturalism*, the idea that what reason can not do, nature will do for us anyway. If reason cannot guarantee us knowledge, nature nevertheless provides us with the good sense to make our way in the world. If reason cannot guarantee morals, our human natures nevertheless supply us with adequate sentiments to behave rightly toward one another. But if reason cannot justify the belief in God and the religious prejudices that go along with it, then so much the worse for religion. Hume was an unrepentant atheist. If the learned tomes of Scholasticism did not succeed in providing sound arguments or good evidence for religious beliefs, then "commit them to the flames," pronounced Hume, infuriating the theologians. Luckily, he did not prescribe the same harsh treatment for other unprovable beliefs, such as our belief in the existence of the "external" world and our belief in the importance of morals. Reason may have its limits, but our sentiments and our natural common sense, cultivated through our social traditions, have power and virtue too. Hume reminds us (again) of what has long been neglected in the search for rational certainty that defined so much of modern philosophy.

Philosophy and Revolution

John Locke was also a great political thinker, and his two treatises on government established the language of basic rights, including the freedom of expression, religious tolerance, and the freedom to own private property. These would become the focal point of revolutions in both the British American colonies (1776) and France (1789), and a revolution in social thinking more basic than either of them.

Locke's theory of natural rights is especially powerful because, instead of making ownership, mutual tolerance, and freedom the product of prior agreement between people, a "social contract," these rights precede all such agreements. A person has the right to a piece of property, for example, because he (or she) "mixes his labor with it." The purpose of contractual agreements, including a constitution and laws of property, is to guarantee those rights. But the rights themselves belong to us by nature. They are "inalienable." They cannot even be given (or sold) away.

The idea that a person was entitled to property, not by law or custom but by natural right, provided the solid foundation for what would come to be called capitalism, although it might be worth noting that

Locke by no means defended excess or unlimited acquisition. The Protestant revolution had already provided the "work ethic" that legitimized a worldly emphasis on success. The Industrial Revolution made such success possible on an enormous scale. A number of philosophers—Locke, Hobbes and others—defended the concept of a "social contract," further destroying traditional authority (such as "the divine right" of rulers) and supporting the new emphasis on democracy and individuality. The new-found wealth of the New World provided the fuel for one of the greatest economic revolutions in history. Like all revolutions, it was both stimulated and spurred on by philosophical ideas.

Voltaire and Rousseau were the two most famous and influential philosophers of the French Enlightenment. *Voltaire* (François-Marie Arouet de, 1694–1778) admired the English Enlightenment and Locke's political philosophy. He imported both back to France, using them to attack both the French government and the Catholic Church. This elegant, self-styled *philosophe* did not write what most people think of as philosophy; he preferred to express himself in polemical essays, political commentary and criticism, and imaginative stories and fables. But Voltaire defended reason and individual autonomy more persuasively than any other philosopher in his society, and he delighted in pricking the hot-air balloons of metaphysics and theology. In this he set the stage for Hume, many years his junior, and he set in motion the middle-class (or, more accurately, *bourgeois*) demands for reform, which would set the stage for revolution in France.

Jean-Jacques Rousseau (1712–1778) was a more subtle and complex thinker who, unlike his older contemporary, did not shy away from grand theories of human nature and society. His early essays, in which he challenged the alleged benefits of "civilization" and defended the life of contentment in an abundant and very un-Hobbesian state of nature, made him famous and began to shake up the staid and self-satisfied aristocracy of Europe. In such books as *Emile* and *The Social Contract,* Rousseau elaborated his theory of human nature as "basically good" and his conception of human society, in which we do not band together to gain mutual security (as Hobbes had suggested) but rather come together to realize our "higher" moral natures. Children should be educated "naturally," he argued, allowed to develop this higher sense in their own way at their own pace, not straitjacketed into the often "unnatural" mores of society. As "citizens" and as participants in the "General Will" of society, we are free to impose the law on ourselves and, even in the context of society, we remain independent, as we once were in nature. But if someone were to refuse to participate, Rousseau ominously suggests, it might be necessary to "force him to be free."

Happy as it may have been, the state of nature was no place to cultivate and exercise the human virtues. Here Rousseau's views hark back to Aristotle. Accordingly, Rousseau finds no contradiction in his attempt to retain both our natural sense of independence and our mutual commitment to make and to obey the laws of society. Nevertheless, our original entry into society was itself neither willful nor happy. From our independence and contentment in the state of nature, humanity took a fall. A catastrophe took place, which was the beginning of society as we know it and the beginning of our unhappiness: someone fenced off a piece of property and declared, "This is mine!" From the establishment of private property came the whole litany of inequalities and injustices that have ruled human life.

In his condemnation of private property, Rousseau could not be more opposed to Locke, and in the battle for the minds of Europe and America, the two would often appear in confrontation. In America, already a land of landowners, lawyers, farmers, and businessmen, it was clear that Locke would win out. In recently feudal France, Rousseau had an evident appeal. But in both revolutions, the Enlightenment assumption was the reality and importance of natural rights and personal independence, guaranteed by the social contract.

The social contract is not, of course, an actual historical event. It is a philosophical fiction, a metaphor, a certain way of looking at society as a voluntary collection of agreeable individuals. The terms of the social contract, accordingly, define the ideal society as one in which we willingly impose the law on ourselves. We are self-governing, and, as in the state of nature, we remain free and independent, without sacrificing the blessings of nature.

Thus the central Western ideal of individual autonomy was rendered compatible with the legitimacy of the state, and the ideal of the natural goodness of humanity replaced the age-old notion of "original" human sin. Then came the American and French Revolutions. Both were, in part at least, revolutions of ideas, upheavals provoked not only by bad government but by ideas of justice and injustice, ideas about the nature of society and about human nature, too.

In America, Thomas Jefferson (1743–1826) took up a number of concepts from Europe, in particular from Locke and the Scottish

Enlightenment. As the primary author of the American Declaration of Independence, Jefferson happily included the idea of self-evident truths (self-evident, that is, to those who know how to see them) and the idea of natural human rights including the rights to life, liberty, private property, and "the pursuit of happiness." With Jefferson, a new invention, "the people," became central to politics. Self-reliance became the primary civic virtue, and it became the responsibility of government to make sure that everyone has sufficient education and property to allow the development of a self-reliant civic character. Education thus becomes not a privilege but an individual right and a political necessity. Religious freedom became a matter not just of mutual toleration but of rights and social tranquility. Government could no longer appeal to divine privilege or mere might but required popular legitimacy.

The Declaration was not only a justification of revolt against English colonial rule. It was also a spectacularly well-crafted endorsement of Enlightenment principles. The revolution was not only a rejection of "taxation without representation"; Americans have not shown much love of taxation even with representation. It was a vision of an entirely new form of government, one that, as a later American President would with equal eloquence sum it up, is "of the people, by the people and for the people."

The American War of Independence was hardly a "revolution" in the sense that revolutions literally turn things upside-down. It was the comparatively untraumatic booting out of a government already far removed and somewhat indifferent to its troublesome New World holdings. In France, by contrast, what began as a shift of power (from the aristocracy to the *bourgeoisie*) turned into a firestorm. Every aspect of life and every part of the country was profoundly affected, torn apart, threatened, and seduced with promises. Conservatives around the world were horrified.

The revolution began with a Declaration of Rights, including the right to life and the right to resist oppression. Thomas Jefferson, visiting Paris as the American ambassador, predicted a gradual improvement in the monarchy and the establishment of a truly representative government. The creation of a National Assembly, representing all classes, promised to introduce cooperation and harmony in place of bitter class divisions. By 1792, however, the revolution had taken a violent turn. Representatives of "the people" fomented local uprisings and turned the country into a bloodbath. Maximilien Robespierre and Jean-Paul Marat, devoted followers of Rousseau, pushed to implement their mentor's notion of a "General Will" on a populace that seemed primarily set on historical revenge. The King and then the Queen were executed by guillotine. Then followed the "Terror," which would eventually claim the lives of its own Rousseauian architects. In 1795, France was on the verge of anarchy within and invasion by its neighbors when appeared a young Corsican colonel named Napoleon Bonaparte. By 1800, the Enlightenment and its ideals were about to begin a new chapter.

Adam Smith and the New World of Commerce

That new chapter had to do not only with a new era of warfare, but also the Industrial Revolution. The new commercialism had been changing the face of Europe since the Renaissance. Even the Church, long hostile to commerce in general and to usury (profitable moneylending) in particular, shifted its ground. The Calvinist reformation encouraged the new commercial consciousness. The new economic order, already in full swing with the Industrial Revolution in England, needed a proper philosophy.

Adam Smith (1723-1790) was David Hume's best friend and closest colleague. What Smith shared with Hume was a love of history and literature and a conservative concern for the nature of what we would now call liberal society, with its definitive (if controversial) institution of private property. Most of all, Smith shared with his friend Hume a deep sense of the ultimate importance of ethics and an understanding of human nature. He is best known as the father of the free-enterprise system, and the author of the "bible" of capitalism, *An Inquiry into the Causes of the Wealth of Nations* (1776). It was the beginning of modern economics and of what we might call the philosophy of the free market system.

In *Wealth of Nations*, Smith gave a partial defense to the long-demeaned concept of self-interest. The law of "supply and demand" assures us that, with time, the best and cheapest products will earn the richest rewards, and the overall interests of both consumer and manufacturer will be optimized. It was a simple idea, elegant and radical. Self-interest could serve the public good. This did not mean that self-interest should now be considered a virtue, however, and there was nothing in Adam Smith to support a "Greed is good" mentality. Still, one can easily imagine what a breath of fresh air the citizens of the late eighteenth century must have experienced when they were told, after two millennia of carping on the evils of money and the sins of avarice, that self-interest had its benefits, not just for one but for all. To the delight of novice entrepreneurs, Smith also argued that government, which had hitherto controlled or regulated virtually every major commercial transaction, should not interfere with the economy. "*Laissez faire*," was the language of the day, "Leave us alone." Smith's proposals also meant that the guilds and guild-like corporations would no longer monopolize industry. Enterprise would now be "free."

On the basis of *Wealth of Nations*, Smith has been widely cited (mainly by those who have not read him) as the classic defender of commercial individualism, of power and profit. The truth is that Smith, years before he wrote *Wealth of Nations*, published an account of human nature in terms of the moral sentiments, distinctively human *feelings* that moved men and women to live harmoniously together in society. Thus, despite the booming thesis of *Wealth of Nations*, Smith believed that people are not essentially selfish or self-interested but are essentially social creatures who act out of sympathy and fellow-feeling for the good of society as a whole. A decent free-enterprise system would only be possible in the context of such a society.

The new modern world would be defined, to a large extent, by the new commercial society and the language of rights and the individual. There may be limits to human knowledge, but there seemed to be no limit to the human prospect. Humanism had reasserted itself so powerfully that it was difficult to remember its alternatives. Protagoras, in that sense, had proved to be right. But there would prove to be limits to humanism as well.

Part III

From Modernity
to Postmodernism

The Domain(s) of Reason: Kant

In Germany, the Enlightenment (or *Aufklärung*) was greeted with some suspicion, and the French Revolution was viewed with horror. The Enlightenment was rightly viewed not so much as a universal or cosmopolitan philosophy as a projection of the reigning ideas in London and Paris, a bit of intellectual imperialism. The Revolution in Paris was not viewed as the triumph of philosophy but rather as the eruption of chaos, and it would still be more than a decade before the fruits of the Enlightenment would seriously affect most Germans.

Nevertheless, the ultimate philosophical champion of the Enlightenment would emerge in Germany. *Immanuel Kant* (1724–1804) was a follower of Leibniz as well as an enthusiastic follower of Newton's physics and Rousseau's radical new theories of society and education. Unlike most of his countrymen, Kant was also an enthusiastic supporter of the French Revolution, albeit from a very safe distance in East Prussia. But what got him most involved in the Enlightenment project was a different revolution, one that began with his encounter with David Hume's skepticism.

Hume's skepticism awakened Kant from his "dogmatic slumbers," that is, his uncritical acceptance of Leibnizian metaphysics. Kant now recognized the limits as well as the power of reason, and his culminating works in philosophy, accordingly, were three great *Critiques* of reason and judgment. But the critique of reason had broad implications beyond philosophy. Historically, Kant redefined the confrontation between religion and science, a conflict that had been growing more acute since the Middle Ages. Kant was a devout Christian, a Pietist Lutheran, and his faith was unshakable. He was also a firm believer in the new physics of Isaac Newton. Kant therefore insisted that we must "limit knowledge to make room for faith." "Two things fill me with awe," he wrote, "the starry skies above and the moral law within." Kant's basic move in philosophy was to separate the starry skies and the moral law (along with religion), and to search for reason in (and beyond) both of them.

Nevertheless, neither science nor morality and religion are limited *within* their own separate spheres. The basic principles of science—which Hume had questioned with his skepticism—would be shown to be "universal and necessary," or what Kant called *a priori*. At the same time, the realm of God and the immortality of the human soul, together with human freedom and moral obligation, would not be compromised by science. Causality and the substantial world of science had their place as *phenomenon*, the world of our experience. But the great ideas Kant summarized as "God, Freedom and Immortality" (morality, too) had their world as well, an "intelligible" world, a world independent of experience but, nevertheless, equally ruled by reason.

Reason, the watchword of the Enlightenment, was the primary player in Kant's supremely rational philosophy. Science would be demonstrated, against the efforts of Hume, to be rationally justified. Morality would be shown to consist of universally obligatory moral laws. Even faith, so often taken to be the epitome of irrationality (or, at least, beyond reason) would be defended as rational, justifiable belief. Kant's strategy was to distinguish the realm of experience from that which transcended experience, or what was usually called "metaphysics." The reason why the problems of metaphysics seemed irresolvable, he suggested, was because the limits of knowledge are the limits of experience, and metaphysical problems by their very nature transcend experience. Some of these questions, notably those all-important questions concerning God, freedom, and immortality, could be answered, but not as matters of knowledge. They were matters of reason, but *practical* reason. They were "postulates of morality" and not like truths of science.

The problems of knowledge and the foundations of science are addressed in what many philosophers take to be the greatest single book in philosophy, Kant's magnificent *Critique of Pure Reason*, first published 1781. According to Kant, we "constitute" the objects of our experience out of our intuitions or sensations, locating those objects in space and time and in causal relationships with other objects. Without the concepts of the understanding, Kant famously suggests, our intuitions would be blind. But without sensations, he says, our concepts would be empty. Experience is always the application of the understanding to sensations, and the world as we know it is the result.

Some of our concepts, however, are not derived from experience (are not, that is, "empirical") but rather *precede* experience. They are *a priori*, part of the built-in structure, or, if you prefer, the basic rules of the human mind. These rules are called "categories." The category of substance, for example, is the rule governing every human experience which requires that sensations be organized in such a way that they are experienced as material objects. Here is Kant's response to Hume's skepticism. The external world is not inferred from our experience but, as a basic category of our thinking and perceiving, is essential to the constitution of our experience. Not all of the most basic or *a priori* structures of the mind are categories. There are also *a priori* "forms of intuition," space and time. The discovery of space and time as *a priori* forms of intuition allowed Kant to make an even more radical suggestion concerning the nature of mathematics and geometry, those disciplines whose necessity had so impressed the Greeks and that modern philosophers had more or less taken for granted as "truths of reason." The propositions of arithmetic and geometry, according to Kant, are necessarily true because they are formal descriptions of the *a priori* structures of time and space, respectively.

Kant's new "idealism" (the view that the world is constituted by our ideas) was, needless to say, an extremely radical view of our knowledge of the world. Without going quite so far as to say that we actually create our world (a thesis that some of the Romantic post-Kantians would happily endorse), Kant suggested that we do not in any sense have to infer or prove the existence of the world "outside of" us. But if we organize or "constitute" our world, can we not do so as we please? The answer, according to Kant, is flatly "no!" We do not choose the sensations that form the basic material of our experiences, nor can we choose any alternative to three-dimensional space and irreversible, one-dimensional time. Nor could there be different sets of categories, different ways of organizing, interpreting, or "constituting" our experience. The categories that form the basic structures or rules of the mind are universal and necessary. This is a remarkable combination of radical rethinking and conservative support of common sense and the scientific view of the world.

Kant denies that the world is outside of our experience, but he also denies that the objects of the world are *in* our experience, that is, "in us." They are, by their very nature as objects, outside of the self. What, then, is the self? The self is, first of all, an activity, or an enormous set of activities, imposing the categories on sensations received, and coming to understand the world. This self is not a thing, a "soul," or even a "mind," but is rather the *transcendental ego*, and its operations are inherent and recognizable in every experience. It is what Descartes recognized, but then misconceived, as the "thinking thing" that he took to be himself.

There is also that more ordinary conception of oneself as a person, as an embodied, emotional intelligence with features, friends, a history, a culture, a context. This is what Kant calls the *empirical* self. It is known, like anything else in the world, through experience. But in addition to the transcendental and empirical selves, there is also what we might awkwardly call "the self in-itself." This is the self that acts as an agent, the self that deliberates and acts, the self that is moral or immoral, responsible or irresponsible, the self that lives at the heart of the practical world.

In his second *Critique*, the *Critique of Practical Reason*, Kant discussed morality, human freedom, and the basic beliefs of any rational religion. Morality—the universal obligations of the moral law—depends on the *will*. Every person has a rational will, and this will is *free*. It is not part of the phenomenal world. Thus we are able to resist inclinations (desires, emotions, and so on) and we can regulate our behavior in accordance with our own law, the law that reason constructs for itself, the moral law. According to Kant, we demonstrate our freedom precisely when we act in accordance with this moral law. We are unfree, on the other hand, when we simply follow the causal dictates of nature (our inclinations).

Because we all have the same faculty of reason within us, Kant was convinced that we will all reach the same conclusions regarding morality. The moral law is primarily concerned with the moral demand to resist our inclinations. In general, reason tells us that we should resist inclination when we cannot endorse the same type of behavior on the part of others in similar circumstances. A moral principle is one that allows this form of impersonal universalization, what Kant calls the *categorical imperative*. (In fact, Kant formulates a number of such imperatives, but he contends that these are merely alternative "formulations," dictating the same moral conclusions.)

Kant's ethical theory, with its emphasis on human freedom, does not explain morality in religious terms. In fact, Kant was adamant in his insistence that morality must provide its own justification, not depend on religious sources or sanctions. Thus, although Kant himself was quite religious, his moral theory was compatible with a secular or atheistic perspective. Yet, Kant wanted to establish room for faith along with freedom. He argued that faith is basic to our rational motivation, demonstrating what Kant's hero Rousseau had called "a moral vision of the world." Without faith, our experiences of injustice are bound to discourage us away from morality. In order to persist in our commitment to morality, we need to believe that, ultimately, moral behavior converges with happiness. And it is not enough for this to be "wishful thinking." Like morality itself, it must be a rational belief. This leads us to "postulate" the existence of God, the immortality of the human soul, and an afterlife. Reason, but not as knowledge, points us in the direction of religious faith.

Kant pursued this relationship between our mental faculties and the natural world, but in a quite different way, in his third *Critique*, the *Critique of Judgment*. There he considered the nature of aesthetic experience, especially our experience of the *beautiful*, and examines the apparent conflict between two commonly held views about aesthetic taste. On the one hand, there seems to be no way to adjudicate disputes about taste, which seems to be purely subjective. On the other hand, we generally expect others to agree with our judgments of taste. Kant reconciles the tension between the two by claiming that the experience of beauty is *universally subjective*. As a person's experience, it is subjective, occasioned by the "free play" of the imagination and the understanding. This activity is inherently enjoyable, and it is also profound. It is not undertaken, like most of our other activities, with any further purpose in mind, but simply for its own sake. We are also justified in assuming that our aesthetic experiences of beauty have a universal aspect, since anyone can use his or her cognitive faculties to enjoy them.

Kant also considered the experience of the *sublime*, the aesthetic appeal of objects that are too massive or too dynamic to be fully comprehensible to the human faculties—for example, the expanse of the starry skies or the violent rush of Niagara Falls. Our enjoyment in these cases, Kant claims, is based on our recognition that reason is able to master such recalcitrant "objects" by conceiving of infinity — even though our imaginations are inadequate to encompass the spectacle. We gain a further sense of our dignity as rational beings in this way, while at the same time experiencing our relative insignificance in the natural scheme of things. The sublime, together with the beautiful as a sense of purpose and order, inspire us to think of nature and ourselves as part of an even larger design. This notion of a large design, like Aristotle's teleology, is the sense that every aspect of the phenomenal world has its place in a larger purpose, and this in turn draws our thoughts toward a supersensible reality. Ultimately, Kant believes that the orderliness of nature and the harmony of nature with our faculties guides us toward an even more profound religious perspective, a sense of the world not limited to knowledge and freedom or even to faith, in the ordinary sense of the term. It is a sense of cosmic harmony that anticipates some of the most dramatic philosophical visions of the nineteenth century.

Hegel and History

G. W. F. Hegel (1770–1831) was almost nineteen years old when the French Revolution began, just across the border and not far from his home in Stuttgart. Like many young men in Germany, he had followed the Enlightenment and the events in France with a cautious enthusiasm. The world was changing. The world was becoming "modern." And as Hegel was just beginning his philosophical ascendancy and completing his first book, Napoleon was at the height of his powers, promising (or threatening, depending on your point of view) to unify Europe and initiate a new era of internationalism. In fact, Napoleon's greatest battle took place by the town of Jena, in which Hegel was then teaching. Hegel actually saw Napoleon, whom he would call "world history on horseback," after his victory,

Philosophically, Hegel greatly admired and emulated Kant, but the significance of his philosophy went far beyond the academic battles that were then being fought in Kant's wake. Hegel summarized the trauma and euphoria of his age. He announced the birth of a new world, which was now manifesting itself in philosophy as well as in international politics. Now that the *Weltgeist,* or "World Spirit," was about to enter into this new era, philosophy, too, was about to achieve its final goal, the all-embracing comprehension of history and humanity.

It is often said that Hegel added a dimension to the enterprise of philosophy, namely, its history. To be sure, other philosophers had generously or critically referred to their predecessors, but the idea of a true history of philosophy, that is, the idea of not only philosophy but all of human intelligence as a systematic progression was an exciting idea whose time had come. Hegel's philosophy was a self-conscious attempt to transcend the various distinctions and warring camps that had defined human thought for the past two-and-a-half millennia. All such conflicts must be seen in the larger context of the *Weltgeist,* Hegel insisted, as local scuffles and disagreements rather than as definitive contrasts. Secularism and monotheism, science and spirit, reason and passion, individual and community—all find their place as concepts that are useful yet may come into conflict in a historical *dialectic* that encompasses all of human experience and knowledge.

In 1807, Hegel published his first, and many would say his greatest, book, *The Phenomenology of Spirit.* The *Phenomenology* is a magnificent conceptual odyssey that carries us from the most elementary conceptions of human consciousness to the most all-encompassing and complex. Its stated purpose is to reach the truth—the "absolute" truth—but the term "absolute" does not mean "final and finished," nor does the term "truth" refer to "the facts." What Hegel is after as philosophical truth is an all-encompassing vision, and the arrogant language of the "absolute" is at the same time a kind of grand philosophical humility, the awareness that we are all part of something much greater than ourselves. Our individual contributions to knowledge and the truth can never be definitive but will always be partial, "mediated," and one-sided.

The central concern of the *Phenomenology* is the nature of Spirit (or *Geist*), the idea of a cosmic soul that encompasses all of us and all of nature. The conclusion of the *Phenomenology* is this sense of all-encompassing Spirit. It is not that all disagreements are resolved, all disputes are settled, all questions are answered. It is rather that, no matter how difficult the disagreements, how bitter the disputes, or how unanswerable the questions, we are all in this together. Napoleon only aspired to unify the world. Hegel actually did it—in theory, of course;

but the idea of an all-embracing consciousness is the first step toward achieving actual world unity.

The first part of the *Phenomenology* is concerned with the questions of knowledge that had so obsessed modern philosophy from Descartes to Kant. Hegel accepted Kant's refutation of skepticism but rejected, even in Kant, the atemporal treatment of knowledge and the timeless conception of the categories. Knowledge, Hegel insisted, *develops*. Like Aristotle, Hegel took biology and the organic as his paradigm, not physics and not mathematics. Consciousness is not just the transcendental perspective from which or within which we gain knowledge of the world. Consciousness grows. It develops new concepts and categories. It finds itself torn between one "form of consciousness" and another, and it learns to reconcile them or, in any case, move beyond them. Consciousness and knowledge are dynamic, a dialectic. They grow through confrontation and conflict, not by way of mere observation and understanding.

Consciousness develops into self-consciousness, and Hegel went on to reject the self-reliant self of Descartes and Kant and to argues that the self is socially constructed, created in interpersonal interaction. This problem of selfhood provokes the best-known and most dramatic chapter in the *Phenomenology*, the parable of master and slave. Told in the most stark and minimalist terms, the parable is that two "self-consciousnesses" confront each other and fight for mutual recognition. In a battle that is (almost) to the death, one wins, one loses. One becomes the master, the other the slave. Each gets recognition and thereby identifies himself through the eyes of the other. The point was to show that selfhood develops not through introspection but rather through mutual recognition. That is, the self is essentially social. Hegel was also concerned with showing the true nature of a certain kind of interpersonal relationship presupposed by many philosophers (e.g., Hobbes and Rousseau) in their hypotheses about the "state of nature." The common assumption is that human beings are first of all individuals and only later, by mutual agreement, members of society. Hegel thought this assumption was nonsense, because individuality appears only within an interpersonal context. What people basically want and need is not only security and material necessities but mutual recognition. Any other view of human nature will miss the essential complexity of human existence.

Throughout the *Phenomenology*, Hegel reveals inadequacies in one form of consciousness after another, guiding us from one view or attitude to another. From the unhappy conclusion of the master/slave parable—it turns out that both the master and the slave find themselves in an untenable position—we are led through various philosophical strategies for coping with or evading the difficulties of life (Stoicism, Skepticism, and certain forms of Christianity). When we finally get to Spirit, which is the beginning of the long culmination of the *Phenomenology*, we come to understand that not only do we mutually define ourselves through recognition and the roles that we play, but we also identify ourselves, ideally, all together. We do this through our sense of ourselves as a moral community and through religion. A dead-end in the dialectic is the French Revolution, which Hegel used as an illustration of how uncontrolled individual freedom ends only in self-destruction. It is in reaction to this excessive individuality that Hegel then turned to a more "communitarian" sensibility, from which he would evolve his political philosophy. Ultimately, we are all one Spirit; recognizing this all-important truth is the "absolute" end of Hegel's philosophy.

Hegel's *System of Logic* (which is not a logic in the formal, mathematical sense) focused on that basic set of concepts or "categories" that Kant had defended as the *a priori* basis of all knowledge. Where Kant had defended a rigidly ordered, neatly defined set of such categories, Hegel was concerned with demonstrating the "fluidity" and mutually defining nature of such concepts. Concepts are always contextual; their meaning depends on their contrasts and complements. And concepts are ultimately intelligible only on the basis of experience. Snatched out of context and merely formalized, they have no real meaning at all. Indeed, the whole point of Hegel's *Logic* is ultimately to show the futility of that movement in modern philosophy that so insists on distinguishing merely subjective experience from objective reality and knowledge. The inseparability of knowledge, reality, and experience has been brought home in this century by virtually every work in contemporary physics.

In his later years, when he was the best-known philosopher in Germany and Professor at the great University of Berlin, Hegel expanded and completed his philosophy in his lectures. He developed a philosophy of nature, simplified his logic and added to it a comprehensive history of philosophy, in effect inventing the subject as we know it today. But perhaps Hegel's most important and most controversial contribution to philosophy was his political vision and his view of modern society.

Hegel's interest in politics went back to his earliest lectures in Jena at the turn of the century, when Napoleon was making his way across Europe and instigating revolutions in the fragmented German states. His politics and social theory were suggested in the *Phenomenology*, and they emerged in his concise *Philosophy of Right*, written in 1821, only six years after the fall of Napoleon and at the onset of that stable but oppressive period in European history often called "the Reaction." Needless to say, Hegel's views were affected by this turbulent history. In the *Phenomenology*, Hegel had buoyantly announced his philosophy as a "new sunrise." The *Philosophy of Right*, by contrast, begins by saying "the owl of Minerva [the Roman goddess of wisdom] flies only at twilight," suggesting that philosophy comes after the fact merely to describe what has already happened. By its very nature, Hegel implied, philosophy is a conservative discipline.

The controversial aspect of Hegel's political philosophy was his view that the individual is secondary to the state. His target was the whole history of social and political thought stretching back to Hobbes and the Enlightenment, but his was not the totalitarian or authoritarian vision that it is sometimes said to be. Hegel should not be confused with certain later philosophers (Lenin and Mussolini, for example) who made bad work of Hegel's point that the significance of the individual is dependent on the social context in which he or she lives. In fact, Hegel argued that the whole point of human history, its ultimate teleology, is the realization of human freedom.

The Battle between Poetry and Philosophy: Romanticism

At the turn of the nineteenth century, German philosophy might have appeared to be preoccupied with a small number of gigantic questions, beginning with the possibility of human knowledge and ending with the eventual seizure of "the Absolute." But within that thin, if cosmic, framework were a number of lively disputes, not only between (what Schopenhauer would call) "irritable philosophy professors" but among the most gifted poets and prophets of the age. All wanted to be the *Dichter* of the new Germany—not just a poet but a sage, the spokesperson for the spirit of the age. Thus competition arose, not only between the irritable philosophy professors but also between the philosophers and the poets, between reason and soul.

Plato's ancient quarrel with the poets came alive again in Germany, except that this time, the philosophers were on the defensive.

The hard-fought battle for the objectivity of reason was challenged by the modern cults of passion and genius, the misshapen but enthusiastic movement we generally know as *Romanticism*. The Enlightenment, or *Aufklärung,* had never dominated Germany in the way that it had pervaded both England and France. Insofar as the Germans looked westward for enlightenment, it was not Hume who awakened them but rather Rousseau, with his comforting fantasies of natural independence and benign sentimentality. The emerging champion of the new German spirit was a *Dichter* named Johann **Herder** (1744–1803). Herder was also a philosopher (and we should take care not to fall into the trap of exaggerating the differences between philosophy and poetry), but he was a philosopher of a very different temperament. Unlike Kant and the Enlightenment, which claimed to be "cosmopolitan" and universal, Herder complained, even as a young man, that such a philosophy made him feel "homeless." For him and in part because of him, German culture and particular German ideas had a right to their own special place on the world stage.

Unlike Kant and the Enlightenment, which championed reason, Herder emphasized feeling, *Gefühl*, immediate experience. It was through feeling that we were initially one with the world, through which we came to recognize our own "vital powers." Consciousness and language ruptured that original unity. This was not in itself a bad thing, but the life of reflection was a limited life. The life of feeling, the "storm and stress" captured by poetry, was essential to being a whole person at one with the world.

Decades before Hegel, Herder believed in history. In this, he was the German incarnation of another neglected genius, an Italian named *Giambattista Vico* (1668–1744), who died the year Herder was born. Both Herder and Vico went against the grain of virtually the whole philosophical tradition, which tended to ignore history and culture and treat the truth as a timeless, changeless reality. Vico bitterly attacked Descartes, his rationalism, and his method of deduction. Like Herder, he appreciated the importance of the irrational in life, and he emphasized the role of religious faith and obedience, as opposed to philosophical reflection, as the essential ingredient in social life. Both Herder and Vico were early opponents of technology, or at any rate felt very uneasy about the new celebration of the machine. Like Rousseau, they challenged the general Enlightenment wisdom that praised science and technology for its improvement of human life.

Prompted by a youthful enthusiasm for the work of his country-man Machiavelli, Vico recognized the sad but obvious fact that human life tended to be defined not by reason but by discord, by conflict, by change. Thus Vico defended an evolutionary vision of history, stages of social growth much like the stages of growth of an individual. But like an individual, a society too can become cor-rupted and decadent, and die. Herder employed the same analogy but included a bit more idealism, holding out for a "higher unity." This became the definitive image of Romanticism: unity emerging out of discord and conflict, universality emerging out of particularity, God and the absolute emanating from the complexity and confusion of everyday life. In this vision, at least, Hegel can be counted among the Romantics. (Hegel denied the affiliation.)

Both the rationalists and the Romantics traced their ideas back to Kant, whose taste in poetry tended toward the limerick and whose taste in music could be satisfied by a Sunday-afternoon military-band concert. But the Kant who so excited the Romantics was not the Kant who had been awakened by Hume and who took on the chal-lenge of defending the foundations of Newton's physics. Nor, in fact, was it the Kant who defended the "categorical imperative" and the universality of the moral law. It was rather the Kant of the third Cri-tique, *The Critique of Judgment*, which was concerned with aesthetic judgment and the purposefulness of the cosmos, who so intrigued them. What captured the imagination and the *hubris* of the young Romantic poets of Germany was Kant's apparent suggestion that the purpose of the world was to be found in art and in the spontaneous promptings of *genius*. (One of the inevitable consequences of that idea was a lot of bad poetry.)

What the young Romantics were lacking was a true romantic philosopher, someone who would follow Kant's genius but tailor the world to suit their cosmic and typically tragic sensibilities. It would not hurt, however, if he also had a good and wry sense of humor. That philosopher was *Arthur Schopenhauer* (1788–1860). Schopen-hauer is best known for his pessimism and his curmudgeonly style. His antipathy toward Hegel was profound. What Schopenhauer most despised in Hegel was his optimism, his sense that humanity was improving. Schopenhauer thought that most people, most of the time, were completely deluded, and that this had not changed much since the human race began. A great admirer of Kant, he utilized Kant's notion of the phenomenal world to adopt the Buddhist idea that the world is illusion. Schopenhauer was perhaps the first great philosopher to import wholesale the ancient teachings of Asia, and the core of his philosophy, in opposition to Hegel's self-consciously rational optimism, was the first "noble truth" of Buddhism: life is essentially suffering.

Insofar as we consider ourselves part of the world, we ignore the profound reality that underlies it, the "thing-in-itself" that is *Will*. For Kant, of course, the Will is essentially rational and presupposes freedom. Schopenhauer departed from Kant by denying the rationality of the Will and by denying that the Will is peculiar to individual human agents. There is but one Will, and it underlies everything. Every being in the phenomenal world manifests the Will in its own way: as a natural force, as instinct, or, in our case, as intellect. In each case, the same inner reality is expressed, and in every case, there can be no satisfaction. The Will is ultimately without purpose. An animal is born. It struggles to survive. It mates, reproduces, and dies. Its offspring do the same, and the cycle repeats itself generation after generation. What could be the point of all of this? And are we, as rational creatures, any different?

Following the Four Noble Truths of Buddhism, Schopenhauer contended that all of life is suffering. Suffering is caused by desire, and we can alleviate suffering, as the Buddhists taught, by "ending all selfish desire." Schopenhauer, like the Buddhists, recommends asceticism. But the most ready palliative for us, according to Schopenhauer, is aesthetic experience. Art allows us a "Sabbath from the penal servitude of willing." Schopenhauer insisted that the artist of genius transforms both beholder and object. The young Romantics were delighted. They had found their champion.

Beyond Hegel: Kierkegaard, Feuerbach, and Marx

Schopenhauer was not Hegel's only philosophical antagonist. *Søren Kierkegaard* (1813–1855) was another. Kierkegaard was born and raised in Copenhagen, where the rationalist influence of Kant and Hegel absolutely dominated the Lutheran church, which in turn dominated the whole of Danish life. Against the rational reconstructions of religious faith in Kant, Kierkegaard insisted that faith was by its very nature irrational, a passion rather than a provable belief. Against Hegelian holism, which synthesized all of humanity, nature, and God into a single Spirit, Kierkegaard insisted on the primacy of "the individual" and the profound "Otherness" of God. And against the worldly Lutherans, carrying out their business as usual and treating church as part of the weekly ritual, Kierkegaard preached a stark, passionate, solitudinous, and unworldly religion that, in temperament at least, would "go back into the monastery out of which Luther broke." Kierkegaard's task in life, a Socratic task, he insisted, was to redefine "what it means to be a Christian."

In defining this new sense of Christianity, Kierkegaard gave a rather spectacular interpretation to the otherwise banal concept of *existence* and insisted on the importance of passion, free choice, and self-definition. Existence, according to Kierkegaard, is not just "being there" but living passionately, choosing one's own existence and committing oneself to a certain way of life. Here is the beginning of **existentialism**. Such existence is rare, he says, for most people simply form part of an anonymous "public" in which conformity is the rule.

Kierkegaard's own chosen way of life was Christianity, which he distinguished with great irony and frequent sarcasm from the watered-down beliefs and social hand-holding of "Christendom." To be or become a Christian, according to Kierkegaard, it is necessary to passionately commit oneself, to make a "leap of faith" in the face of the "objective uncertainty" of religious claims. One cannot know or prove that there is a God; one must passionately choose to believe. At the heart of Kierkegaard's philosophy was his emphasis on "subjective truth." Thus he criticized Hegel, with his long view of history and his all-encompassing concept of Spirit, as "an abstract thinker" who completely ignored "the existing, ethical individual." In choosing the religious life, for example, Kierkegaard insisted that there are no ultimately rational reasons, only subjective motives: a sense of personal necessity and passionate commitment. One must "leap." There are no guarantees.

BY THE MIDDLE of the nineteenth century, there seemed to be no alternative to idealism in German philosophy. The world was constituted by ideas, whether the world was thereby an illusion (as in Schopenhauer) or transcendentally objective (as in Kant) or even absolute (as in Hegel). Then into the German philosophical world marched an iconoclast named *Ludwig Feuerbach* (1804–1872), who had first made his scandalous reputation with a book that was harshly critical of Christianity. Feuerbach's down-to-earth materialism can be summarized in his famous line (and infamous pun), "you are what you eat." (*"Man ist was Man isst."*) So much for the idealistic constitution of the world. What a philosopher eats for dinner, and, more generally, how one physically copes with the world, defines one's life. The ideas merely follow.

AFTER HEGEL'S DEATH in 1831, his philosophy, coupled with the radical new materialism of Feuerbach, provided inspiration for a new generation of politically rebellious students, who saw in a Feuerbachian interpretation of Hegel's "dialectic" a way of understanding history and political conflict. The most famous of these young materialist Hegelians was *Karl Marx* (1818–1883), who began his career as a Romantic poet and polemical journalist but then turned to converting Hegel's dialectic of ideas into a theory about the power of economics. In place of Hegel's World Spirit were the forces of production. In place of ideas in confrontation were competing socioeconomic classes.

History has always been filled with class conflict, Marx told us, between the "haves" and the "have-nots." This was true of the master-slave relationships of the ancient world and the manor lords and their serfs in feudal times. In the modern industrial age, it has become a conflict between the owners or "entrepreneurs" and their workers, between the *bourgeoisie* and the *proletariat*. But just as Hegel had shown how a way of thinking or a way of life can fail due to its own internal contradictions, Marx argued that the "capitalist" way of life, which pits a few wealthy industrialists against a mass of exploited subsistence workers, would collapse of its own internal contradictions. Ultimately, Marx, predicts, this collapse will result in a "classless society," in which work and its rewards will be equitably shared, no one will be exploited, and no one will suffer the deprivations of poverty.

Marx's utopian vision would eventually become one of the most powerful ideologies in the world, even surviving the worldwide collapse of communism in the 1990s. Whatever one may think of the Marxist dream compared to the free-enterprise system defended by Adam Smith (and one should not underestimate the extent to which the two are sometimes in agreement—for example, on the intrinsic worth of human labor and in a contempt for monopolists), the worldly world of economics and a more dynamic conception of materialism had clearly found their way into philosophy.

Where to, Humanity? Mill, Darwin, and Nietzsche

In England, the Industrial Revolution was already into its second century. Commerce was booming, and consumerism, hitherto a minor force in the world of economics, was changing the world. The new emphasis on personal satisfaction naturally suggested a new philosophy, a philosophy in which the maximization of personal happiness would become the ultimate end. That philosophy was called *utilitarianism*, and although it had its roots in the eighteenth century, it really hit its stride in the philosophy of its most eloquent spokesman, *John Stuart Mill* (1806–1873).

David Hume had been something of a utilitarian; he had insisted that all ethics had its basis in "utility." *Jeremy Bentham* (1748–1832) had given the movement its first full and official statement as well as its name, and John Stuart Mill's father, *James Mill* (1773–1836), had been one of its more enthusiastic advocates. But it was John Stuart Mill who gave utilitarianism its definitive formulation. Bentham had argued that the essential principle of utility was to maximize pleasure and minimize pain. What Mill adds to this rather crude quantitative theory is the question of the *quality* of pleasure, thus emphasizing the importance of poetry and philosophy despite the fact that, in terms of sheer hedonism, mud wrestling and bowling may give far greater pleasure to those who have not been exposed to more subtle enjoyments. But utilitarianism captured the mentality of the consumer revolution perfectly. With little resistance, it spread into France and, of course, to America where it would find its warmest welcome. In Germany, it was still considered extremely vulgar, but, then, the Industrial Revolution in Germany had hardly begun. (One of Nietzsche's most cutting lines: "Man does not live for pleasure. Only the Englishman does.")

In conjunction with his utilitarianism and his early elaboration of the virtues of free enterprise, Mill also defended a powerful theory of individual rights. His view is a classic statement of "liberalism." Mill later moved closer to socialism, but throughout his career he was an ardent champion of individual liberty. The only reason for limiting any person's freedom, he argued, is in order to protect the freedom of others.

Mill's theory of knowledge was revolutionary, or, rather, a continuation of an older British revolution. His bold new empiricism was especially evident in biology, a field that had long been bounded by Aristotelian categories and religious views about creation. Of course, ever since Aristotle people had been distinguishing the various properties, interactions, and differences between the seemingly endless number of species of animals and plants. The questions of WHY there were so many species and HOW they managed to fit so well into their environment seemed odd. For most people, the traditional answers were provided in Genesis: "because God created them that way." But in the middle of the century, two naturalists (in hot competition), Alfred Russell Wallace (1823–1913) and *Charles Darwin* (1809–1882) proposed a theory that would change the very conception of nature as well as throw some biblical literalists into convulsions.

The theory of *evolution* espoused the idea that species randomly appeared upon the earth over tens or hundreds of millions of years. Depending on their adaptability to their environment, they either survived and reproduced or disappeared. The sticking point of the argument, of course, was the suggestion that human beings had also evolved. Some people were deeply offended by the idea that their great-grandparents had been some sort of ape. Others found it blasphemous to suggest that chance and opportunity, not God, had created the species. But even those who had no problem with the idea of human evolution, like Darwin himself, found themselves facing a momentous question: Could human beings still be evolving? If so, into what? Indeed, could we too be living just some brief, intermediary existence between the "lower" animals and some higher, mightier, or more adaptive creature than ourselves?

IT WAS TOWARD the end of the century that such questions received their most shocking, provocative answers. The German philosopher *Friedrich Nietzsche* (1844–1900) wrote a flamboyant, fictional epic that purported to trace the educational exploits of a character named Zarathustra (after the Persian prophet who had talked about the cosmic forces of good and evil). In *Thus Spoke Zarathustra*, Nietzsche offered up the incredible suggestion that human beings were nothing but a bridge between the ape and the *Übermensch* ("superman"). The future of "human nature" was now called into question.

Alternatively, in the same work, Nietzsche teasingly introduced a character called "the last man," a frightening (or flattering, depending on your point of view) possibility for the "end" of evolution. The last man is the ultimate bourgeois, the satisfied utilitarian, the absolute couch potato. "We have found happiness," says the last man, and he blinks in dull contentment. This, Nietzsche warned, is also one of our possibilities. We can continue to consume our comforts, minimize dangers, ignore the mysterious and unknown, and discourage creativity, until the world is so safe for us that we will become "ineradicable, like the flea." Or, we can strive to become something more than "human, all too human" and aspire to the *Übermensch*. To understand what the *Übermensch* might be, however, we would have to reexamine the whole of Western history to see who we are and how we came to be what we have come to be.

In his insistence that we have to look back to history to appreciate what we are and what we can be, Nietzsche reflected not only Darwin but Hegel, Vico, and Herder. In tracing the evolution of Western thought, he looked back to early Christianity, to Socrates, and even further to Homer and the pre-Socratic dramatists. Nietzsche was by training a classical philologist, and he saw the West's Greek heritage to be in conflict with its Judeo-Christian background. He utterly rejected the "synthesis" of the two that had developed throughout the history of Christianity.

Nietzsche was struck, for example, by the difference between the two traditions' approaches to human suffering. While the Judeo-Christian tradition sought the explanation of misfortune in sin (a kind of "blame the victim" approach, in Nietzsche's view), the ancient Greeks took profound suffering to be an indication of the fundamentally tragic nature of human life. Nietzsche's first book, *The Birth of Tragedy*, analyzed the art of Athenian tragedy as the product of the Greeks' deep unflinching sense of the meaning of life in the face of extreme vulnerability. Tragedy, according to Nietzsche, grew from this recognition and from the beautification, even the idealization, of human fate.

Nietzsche speculated that the Greek view of tragedy integrated two different perspectives, which the Athenians associated with the gods Apollo and Dionysus. Dionysus, the god of wine, sexuality, and revelry, represents the dynamic flux of being, the acceptance of fate, and the chaos of creativity. The devotee takes satisfaction in being part of the wild, unfolding rush of life. From the Dionysian perspective, individual existence is just an illusion; our true reality is our participation in the life of the whole. Apollo, the sun god, on the other hand, reflects the Athenian fascination with beauty and order. From the Apollonian perspective, the individual's existence is undeniably real, and human vulnerability is genuinely horrible. Yet the Apollonian perspective makes this reality appear beautiful, enables us to forget our vulnerability for a time and love our finite lives in the world. The brilliance of Athenian tragedy, according to Nietzsche, was its simultaneous awakening of both perspectives.

Nietzsche vastly preferred this tragic resolution of the problem of evil to the Judeo-Christian resolution in terms of sin and salvation. He also preferred it to the reactive pessimism of his philosophical mentor Schopenhauer and that modern, scientific optimism which ignores the tragic and pretends that all problems that concern us are correctable through technology. Nietzsche applauded the ancient Greeks for their ethical outlook, which stressed the development of personal excellence and nobility, in contrast with what he saw as the Judeo-Christian obsession with sin, guilt, and otherwordly salvation.

Those early Greeks, Nietzsche fantasized, "they knew how to live!" Insofar as the Greeks had a morality, it was based on healthy self-assertion, not self-abasement or the renunciation of the instincts. Enough of the traditional emphasis on "peace of mind" and *apatheia*. Our ideals must be energetic ideals, creative ideals. Like Schopenhauer, Nietzsche contended that human beings, like other beings in nature, are essentially willful, but Nietzsche went further and insisted that we (and all of nature's creatures) are "will to power," driven by the desire to keep expanding our vitality and strength. Against Schopenhauer's pessimism about the meaning of life, Nietzsche insisted that vitality is itself the meaning of life, and that it is the affirmation of life that should be the conclusion of philosophy, not life's rejection.

In contrast with the morality of the ancient Athenians, a morality of tragic heroism and mastery, Nietzsche argued that Christian morality had made the mediocre person with no great enthusiasm into a moral exemplar. The person who does essentially nothing with his or her life but avoides "sin" might merit heaven, on the Christian view, while a creative person will probably be deemed "immoral" because he or she refuses to follow "the herd." According to Nietzsche, many if not most of the prohibitions of Judeo-Christian (and Kantian) ethics are in fact "leveling" devices that the weak and mediocre use resentfully to put more talented and stronger spirits at a disadvantage. Accordingly, Nietzsche defends a view "beyond good and evil," beyond our tendencies to pass moralistic judgments on our own and others' behavior, toward a more creative psychological and naturalistic perspective.

Nietzsche concluded what might be seen as a long progression of attempts to gain access to a transcendent world. He did this by denying, in the most vituperative terms, the very idea of such a world, a reality behind the appearances, a world other than—better than—this one. Nietzsche's attacks on the "otherworldly" had their most obvious target in the Judeo-Christian tradition, with the idea of an all-powerful benign deity behind the scenes. As an antidote to the Christian worldview, which treats human life as a mere beeline to an "eternal" world, Nietzsche advocated a revival of the ancient view of "*eternal recurrence*," the view that time repeats itself cyclically. If one were to take this image of eternal recurrence seriously and imagine that one's life must be lived over and over again in exactly the same way, suddenly there is enormous weight on what otherwise might seem like a mere "moment." In other words, it is life, this life, that alone counts for anything.

Nietzsche's indictments reached beyond Christianity back to Plato, whom he also saw as a proponent of the view that another world is more important than this one. Indeed, Nietzsche's attacks are addressed at virtually the entire Western tradition of philosophy. He sometimes even rejected the very idea of "truth," suggesting that ideas we take to be true are just those beliefs, possibly false ones, that have proven to be useful. Philosophical reflection, too, should give up on the idea of truth and aim instead at living well.

From Puritanism to Pragmatism: Philosophy in America

Nietzsche's rejection of truth in favor of life enhancement would find a certain favor in the New World, itself the subject of considerable philosophical speculation in Europe (now the "Old World"). But American philosophy was a long time finding itself. It is suggestive that one of the first thriving schools of philosophy in America was a group of Hegelians in Saint Louis, Missouri, in the very heart of the country. At Harvard and elsewhere, Germany and Britain provided the dominant philosophical models. Even today, the latest philosophical fashions from New York to California are often imported from France.

The early colonists, however, had more to worry about than European philosophy and fashions. The new settlements were often endangered, and immediate practical reality was an unavoidable preoccupation. American philosophy, accordingly, was defined from its beginnings by a no-nonsense, practical or "pragmatic" sensibility.

The philosophical history of the New World (and, in particular, New England) began, however, with religious squabbles and separatist movements. Many of the early settlers had left Europe in search of religious freedom and tolerance, but (as so often happens) once they found it, they became less than tolerant themselves. The first work of American literature was an attempt to fortify Puritan doctrine, Michael Wigglesworth's "The Day of Doom; or A Poetical Description of the Great and Last Judgment" (1662). The sermons of *Jonathan Edwards* (1703–1758), a New England Puritan minister, were similarly aimed at bolstering religious doctrines. Edwards recalled what he saw as the basic insight of Protestantism, that we are "born depraved" and can find salvation only in God's grace. This religious impulse, and the proliferation of new religious movements, would have much to do with the new American temperament. The Catholic Church in Rome had already lasted more than fifteen hundred years, but the half-life of some New England churches seemed to be a matter of months.

Even when towns and plantations had been settled and money had been made in America, philosophical discipline still seemed to hold little appeal for the busy businessmen and energetic farmers who were pushing into the "wilderness" and sowing the seeds of what later writers would call the great American empire. Nevertheless, there were a number of philosophically talented thinkers in the colonies, mainly lawyers and businessmen. Among them were Thomas Jefferson (1743–1826), the author of the Declaration of Independence, and Benjamin Franklin (1706–1790), who found in the revolutionary ideas of the Enlightenment an ideology (or, more accurately, a complex set of ideologies) upon which to found a new nation. And so, the United States became the land of ideas. It became the first or, in any case, the best-known modern example of a nation founded on a constitution. Nevertheless, American philosophy would find its primary home in the halls of academia, while anti-intellectualism and ignorance of philosophy became increasingly routine even among the educated public.

As America became more industrialized and more urbanized, a Romantic revival rejected comfort and consumerism in favor of a simpler life. In the nineteenth century, with the expansion of industry and the growth of cities in America, philosophers rebelled and celebrated the more sublime aspects of the country's natural beauty. Recently arrived European Americans also developed philosophies focused on nature as a source of spiritual sustenance. And as American cities grew more and more populated and troubled, this fantasy about nature appeared again and again in American thinking. *Henry David Thoreau* (1817–1862) was but the most famous of a long line of self-styled hermits; he took up residence on Walden Pond in Massachusetts. An anarchist without a regular profession, Thoreau praised the simple life of individual communion with nature over the citified lives of commercial venture that attracted so many of his contemporaries. Indeed, his distaste for the excesses of civilized society led him to advocate the tactic of pointed noncooperation as a peaceful means of achieving important social reforms. His essay "Civil Disobedience" has had lasting impact; it inspired both Mohatma Gandhi and Martin Luther King in their movements against imperialism and racial oppression.

Although he was an eccentric, Thoreau was self-consciously part of a larger philosophical movement, *New England Transcendentalism*, which flourished from 1836 until 1860. The great New England "transcendentalists" were direct philosophical descendants of Kant and Hegel. *Ralph Waldo Emerson* (1803–1882), for example, stressed the spiritual importance of Nature. Following Hegel, Emerson also believed that humanity is linked by a collective "Oversoul" that gives intuitive moral guidance. Emerson famously encouraged *self-reliance* as the ultimate virtue, and he conjoined ideas from the Enlightenment and European Romanticism with progressive ideas for social reforms, especially the abolition of slavery and female suffrage. The transcendentalists were optimists, convinced of the inherent goodness of humanity and enthusiastic about its possibilities. It was Emerson who developed the philosophy of *secular humanism*, a philosophy sometimes reviled by contemporary evangelicals. But just as humanism had its origins within the context of the Christian church, secular humanism is based on a religious sensibility.

The transcendentalists were obviously influenced by the European Romantics and idealists, but this intellectual dependency on Europe rightly bothered the American intellectuals of this second full century of American life. Americans had rather self-consciously rejected much else that was distinctly European, and they generally took pride in their own originality and ingenuity. Thus the felt need for a genuine American philosophy. American philosophy would have to be something quite different from the scholastic and metaphysical reflections of Europe. It would involve a uniquely American style of thinking—practical, hard-headed, not scholastic or metaphysical, a reflection of the American experience. This philosophy developed in what was called *pragmatism*.

HARVARD PHILOSOPHER *Charles Sanders Peirce* (1839–1914) advocated his pragmatism as a corrective to the clumsiness and equivocation he found in the scientific method of his day. Peirce was primarily a logician, and he is most famous for developing a theory of signs and their interrelations. Apart from mathematics and the logic of formal signs, he held that supposedly "eternal" beliefs, amenable to *a priori* proof are almost surely of no real use. As a pragmatist, he insisted that we constantly test the reliability of our beliefs, and we discard those that fail the test.

William James (1842–1910), the brother of novelist Henry James, took the hallmark of pragmatism to be a renewed emphasis on *experience*, a "radical empiricism" that would make none of the compromises of the older empiricisms. It was James who coined the phrase "stream of experience," and he lived and worked in what is now the border between philosophy and psychology. He was one of the first Americans to become interested in the new science of neurology, and his two-volume *Psychology*, although obviously dated, is still considered one of the classics in the field. Over and above his scientific interests, however, James was primarily interested in the problems of everyday living. Accordingly, it was he who first popularized pragmatism and brought it out of the halls of Harvard and into the mainstream of American intellectual life. (Peirce, we might note, disdained James's popularization of the movement and came to distinguish his own work by calling it "pragmaticism," "a word so ugly no one else will ever use it.")

Our ideas are of use, James argued, only if they have "cash value," in other words, only if they are actually useful in our practical projects. Good ideas are good for something. But despite this practical emphasis, James did not dismiss the importance of religion or moral beliefs. Indeed, he considered religious experience an indispensable aspect of human "practical" life. Religious experience was more important than religious doctrine, but James also acknowledged that moral and religious beliefs can have "cash value" if they help us to navigate and make sense of our lives.

It is in the context of this emphasis on experience that we can understand the enduring appeal of James in American philosophy, or rather outside of philosophy, for James has often been more celebrated by historians, journalists, and literary critics than by philosophers. "Experience" seems to be just what twentieth-century America is all about, from the continuous invention of new media to the "experience industry" (not just entertainment, but vicarious adventures and well-secured flirtations with danger of every sort). In philosophy, this emphasis on experience also involved a shift toward *pluralism*, the legitimacy of different ways of experiencing and living in the world. It was a perfect philosophy for an increasingly multicultural society of ambitious, adventurous immigrants.

The central figure of twentieth-century pragmatism, and perhaps the definitive American philosopher, was *John Dewey* (1859–1952). Dewey was influenced by the dynamic character of Hegel's vision, and as a young philosopher he was something of an evangelical Hegelian. Although he moved away from Hegel, Dewey built his entire philosophy on a very Hegelian concept of dynamic unity. He was, throughout his career, opposed to all of those exaggerated dualisms—between mind and body, necessary and contingent propositions, cause and effect, secular and transcendent—that split up rather than clarify experience and, in his view, make philosophical progress impossible. He was an anti-reductionist, preferring rich theories and functional understanding—"How does this work?" "How does this fit in?"—to a static, abstract analysis.

Dewey's brand of pragmatism, called *instrumentalism*, treats ideas as tools in our efforts to tackle practical problems. Dewey's emphasis, more than that of any of the other pragmatists, was on *practice*, on the actual ways in which we learn to do things by *doing* them. Thus his theory of education, often ridiculed for its "permissiveness," is first of all the view that children learn by doing, not just by listening or reading. Dewey has many harsh things to say about all of those philosophers who limit their view of human knowledge to a mere "spectator's" perspective, watching, perhaps comprehending but not participating. Thus, in place of traditional philosophy of science, which emphasized method and results, Dewey expanded his vision to explore the nature of inquiry and learning. Education is experience, and experience is the process of problem-solving, participatory and engaged—in other words, just the opposite of the traditional secondary school.

IN A NATION still excusing itself on the grounds that it was "new," some of the greatest philosophers came from the oppressed minorities. We have lost a great deal of the rich oral traditions of native

American Indian philosophy, but we have an eloquent canon of African-American philosophy, articulate cries of protest and some deep thinking about human nature and injustice. *Frederick Douglass* (1817–1895) was a former slave who became the leading orator of the Abolitionist movement. *W. E. B. Du Bois* (1868-1963) analysed the complex character of the American black's sense of identity and defended what was later called "black pride." More recently, *Martin Luther King, Jr.* (1929–1968), defended the idea of a fully integrated society, and in a very different vein, *Malcolm X* (1925–1965) argued against racial oppression. But now we are getting ahead of our story. Before we crossed the Atlantic Ocean to America, we were still back in nineteenth-century Europe. We should go back there, for a great deal is about to happen.

IN AUGUST OF 1900, Nietzsche died. Toward the end of his lucid years, he made some dire prophecies about the new century. This awesome age would experience the terrible realization of the "death of God," the agony of modern decadence and disbelief, the violent consequences of resentment, and the difficult truth that there is, after all, no "truth." Nietzsche predicted a desperate search for new gods or, failing that, *führers*. He predicted a similar search for new myths or, in their place, ideologies. He predicted wars such as the world had never seen. Two world wars (1914–1918, 1939–1945) would, unfortunately, soon prove him prescient.

Back to Basics: Frege, Russell, and Husserl

Philosophy is never isolated or immune from its time and place, no matter how abstract it may be or however "eternal" or "untimely" it may declare itself. Philosophy can be prophetic, it can be nostalgic, or it can act as a mirror, a reflection of a culture. But more often than not, it expresses in abstract terms the ideals and aspirations of society. The Enlightenment was first of all an expression of hope, optimism, and faith in the rational ability of human beings to learn about the world and create a society that would assure peace and prosperity. At the beginning of the twentieth century in Europe, those hopes and good feelings were still very much alive; almost a century had passed since the last all-devouring European war. Nevertheless, the Enlightenment and its attitudes were crumbling, and in the midst of increasing decadence—as Nietzsche had diagnosed in Socrates' Greece of two-and-a-half milennia earlier—philosophy could serve as an escape from the problems of the world. But now, the escape route headed not for the otherworldly but for an ideal world, the pure and precise world of mathematics and logic.

GOTTLOB FREGE (1848–1925) was a politically conservative German mathematician who stimulated the greatly renewed philosophical interest in logic. He attempted to find the "foundations" of arithmetic, deductive proof that such elementary equations, as "two plus two equals four" are indeed necessarily true. He moved logic beyond the study of the relationship between propositions, which had dominated the field since Aristotle, and created the "quantificational" logic (concerned with such categories as "all," "some," "none") that is best known and used by philosophers today. Just as Descartes and Locke started modern philosophy down the royal road of epistemology, Frege steered contemporary philosophy down the road of logic and the analysis of language. It was an exciting breakthrough, this "linguistic turn," and within the bounds of "analytic" philosophy it held open the promise of an all-embracing theory.

In England, a young and extremely liberal aristocrat, *Bertrand Russell* (1872–1970), read Frege. Russell was inspired to prove that the elementary propositions of arithmetic could be demonstrated by using logic alone. (It is said that his interest in doing so was first stimulated when he was a youth of eleven, after the rebellious young genius was told not to question the arithmetic tables but simply to memorize them.) He teamed up with another mathematician of similar inclinations, *Alfred North Whitehead* (1861–1947), and the two produced their formidable, three-volume classic, *Principia Mathematica* (published in 1910–1913), which effectively "reduced" arithmetic to a small set of logical axioms. To this day, there are philosophers who consider only logic to be "real" philosophy.

Russell was a good British empiricist, a scientist and a materialist. He was also an unabashed *atomist*. That is, he believed that simple bits of language—sentences or, more properly, propositions—referred to simple bits of experience—sensations—caused by simple bits of reality—facts. In his theory of knowledge as in his logic, Russell was very much a minimalist. He tried to reduce the complexity of the world and our experience of the world to its simplest "atomic" bits. According to the school he helped establish, philosophy should proceed by way of *analysis*, breaking up the bits and understanding how they fit together. (The British Hegelians, by way of contrast, were always insisting that everything is connected to everything else, and that parts could not be understood without reference to the whole.) Our language, accordingly, would also have to be clarified, improved, *idealized*. We would have to reformulate our grammar according to logic to more accurately reflect the structure of the world.

Later, Russell would turn his attention to other, more worldly matters. He wrote a bestselling book on the history of philosophy and produced a stream of controversial attacks on Christianity and organized religion in general. He publicly defended what would later be called "free love," though in fact he was an outspoken proponent of sexual responsibility. He was a vocal and eloquent opponent of militarism and helped to found the anti-nuclear movement. Toward the end of his long life, he wrote an elegant and impassioned autobiography, conclusively documenting his political commitments, his love of philosophy, and what we might politely call his love of love. He also declared—as the First World War had surely shown—that "the world is horrible." Formal philosophy, by comparison, seemed both a refuge and a waste of time.

Meanwhile, a famously absent-minded Czech-German mathematics professor named *Edmund Husserl* (1859–1938), under the influence of German empiricists, wrote his own philosophy of arithmetic. As opposed to Russell and Whitehead, Husserl argued that the elementary propositions of arithmetic were not based on logic but were rather very abstract generalizations from experience (a thesis argued by John Stuart Mill a few decades before). Frege soundly refuted Husserl, who, in a most unusual move for a philosopher, changed his mind. Husserl then argued, like Russell and Whitehead, that arithmetic was indeed an *a priori* science. But while Russell and Whitehead based their analysis on logic, Husserl was developing an entirely new method of philosophical inquiry into the nature of necessary truth. He would call it *phenomenology*.

Husserl defined phenomenology as the scientific study of the essential structures of consciousness, but phenomenology does not imply a contrast between an appearance and some underlying reality. ("Phenomenology" comes from the Greek word meaning "appearance." Kant had used "phenomenon" to refer to the world of our experience.) By describing those structures, Husserl promised us, we can find certainty, including the foundations of arithmetic, which he sought as a mathematician. To this end, Husserl described a peculiarly phenomenological standpoint in which consciousness is viewed as *intentional*, that is, always directed at some object, whether material or, as in mathematics, "ideal." The phenomenological standpoint is achieved through a series of phenomenological "reductions," which describe these essential features, the *meanings,* of consciousness. Husserl argued that these meanings (like Kant's categories) are universal and necessary, and he rejected the "relativism" that was starting to pervade European (and American) philosophy.

Toward the end of his life, as National Socialism was tightening its grip on Germany and the world was once again preparing for war, Husserl shifted toward a more social and "existential" interest in human knowledge. He warned of a "crisis" in European civilization based on rampant relativism and irrationalism (an alarm that the logical positivists were raising about the same time in Vienna).

The Limits of Rationality: Wittgenstein, Freud, and Weber

In 1911 an extremely intense, brilliant, and wealthy young aristocrat from an old Viennese family showed up on Russell's doorstep in Cambridge. *Ludwig Wittgenstein* was indisputably a genius, and it was not long before Russell admitted that he had taught the young logician everything he had to teach him. Wittgenstein mastered the new logic, adopted his teacher's minimalist and atomistic view of the world, and within a few years transformed philosophy, although not at all as he had intended.

Wittgenstein wrote his *Tractatus Logico-Philosophicus* during the First World War, and when his old teacher Russell finally arranged for its publication in 1921, it was immediately recognized as a philosophical classic. The *Tractatus*, much like some of Nietzsche's books, was a pithy work of carefully ordered and numbered aphorisms. But unlike Nietzsche's always self-questioning books, this one was unashamedly assertive, even dogmatic. It was, or seemed to be, first and foremost a book on logic, a manifesto of classic logical atomism, that is, Russell's picture of minimalist simple sentences that "picture" minimalist simple facts. "The world is everything that is the case," the book begins. Much of the rest is an answer to the question of how sentences (or, more properly, propositions) picture the world.

But the most interesting parts of the book, from a philosophical point of view, have to do with what reason cannot do. Here the influences of Schopenhauer and Nietzsche, as well as several generations of German Romantics, are much in evidence. What reason tries to do but cannot do, is investigate itself. It cannot set, or for that matter even describe, its own limits. ("I am not in my world. I am the boundary of my world.") Nor can one say what is beyond those limits. One cannot say the "unsayable." Beyond the limits of scientific rationality lie the problems of value and questions about values, God, and religion. The end of the *Tractatus* points in this direction: "Whereof one cannot speak, one must be silent." This is not a simple tautology but profound mysticism, silently pointing us toward a multitude of experiences that lie beyond the bounds of philosophy and beyond the limits of reason.

Having said "all that he had to say" in a terse book of less than eighty pages, Wittgenstein left philosophy. He taught school, built a house for his sister, composed some music, and disappeared from Cambridge. But by 1929 he was back, rethinking all that he had done, struggling with not only the new logical forms of philosophy but also the anguish and suffering that had concerned the Stoics and his own predecessors Schopenhauer and Nietzsche. Such topics were virtually absent from the philosophical discussions he had inspired in Cambridge and elsewhere, so soon after he took up a professorship in philosophy at Cambridge ("an absurd profession") he dropped out of academia once again, to put his voluminous new doubts and thoughts together.

After the *Tractatus*, Wittgenstein's philosophy emerged slowly. He clearly rejected logical atomism and the idea of language "picturing" the world. He now argued that the meaning of a sentence depends on how it is *used to do* something. We use sentences in conversations—to communicate, to question, to challenge, to make jokes, to ask for the butter, to talk about philosophy, to tell stories, to argue, to promise and proclaim. Thus the fundamental unit of language is not the simple sentence but the larger *language game*, a "form of life" that may have any number of purposes and goals, many of them having little to do with the search for truth.

Whereas the *Tractatus* maintained a healthy respect, even reverence, for philosophy, Wittgenstein's *Investigations* threatened to turn philosophy into a kind of intellectual malady for which, fortunately or unfortunately, only more philosophy seemed to be the cure. Philosophy thus became a form of therapy.

The search for an all-embracing formal theory also hit a devastating snag in the logic of **Kurt Gödel** (1906–1978). Gödel formulated his "incompleteness proof" in 1931, in which he showed that there will always be some unprovable sentence in any such formal system. The philosophical consequences of this proof are still being debated, but several leading mathematicians and philosophers abandoned the search for an ideal formal language as a result of it.

SIGMUND FREUD (1856–1939) is not usually considered a philosopher, which is surely philosophy's loss and shame. For better or worse, Freud's ideas established the framework for twentieth-century thinking about the mind, human nature, the human condition, and the prospects for human happiness. His anti-Enlightenment ideas that we often do not and cannot know what is going on in our own minds— that we are basically irrational, necessarily unhappy creatures—would become the premise, or at least the problem, for generations of philosophers and social thinkers. On the other hand, Freud's very Enlightenment idea that the mind is ultimately a material entity (namely, the brain), analyzable in terms of neurology, energy circuits, and the language of physics, still defines the science of the mind. So, too, the idea that everything can be explained—even our little "mistakes" and "slips of the tongue," even forgetting and dreaming— remains the underlying supposition of twentieth-century psychology and criticism, not to mention pop psychology.

As always, one can find predecessors for these ideas. The "unconscious" was a topic of discussion for generations of German philosophers, including Nietzsche. What Freud added to this discussion was the concept of *repression*, adding that much of what is repressed is perverse yet psychically active. He outraged the good citizens of the Victorian world by giving them just the sort of explanation of human behavior that they least wanted: that human conduct by its very nature is based on vile, murderous, incestuous motives. So much for the enlightened thesis that human beings are basically good. Sexual perversion (and worse) was everywhere, precariously repressed. Unhappiness was inevitable, and civilization itself was its cause.

IN GERMANY, *Max Weber* (1864–1920), a sociologist, would complement the work of Freud and Wittgenstein in ways that are still not sufficiently appreciated. Weber was particularly concerned with philosophy's favorite topic, *rationality*. Rationality, he argued, had become entrapped in bureaucracy, which, whatever its original blessings, had become something of a curse, devoid of spirituality.

Weber's most famous thesis is that capitalism, and consequently the very structure of modern Western society, is the product of Protestantism. In his *Protestant Ethic and the Spirit of Capitalism*, Weber argues that the harsh Christian philosophy of Calvinism, with its central thesis of predestination, condemned millions of people to unresolvable anxiety. Thus they felt it necessary to "prove" their worth in this life, working feverishly and living ascetically. Of course, no amount of success could possibly quash the anxiety that motivated such energetic entrepreneurship, but with effort and good managment, one could at least make a lot of money.

The Progress of Process: Against Analysis

After completing the *Principia Mathematica* with Russell, Alfred North Whitehead came to America. He also moved away from the formal conception of philosophy and began to doubt, much as Wittgenstein had been doubting, the whole trend of Western philosophy. The purpose of philosophy, he would later insist, is to rationalize mysticism, to "express the infinity of the universe in terms of the limitations of language," and gain "direct insight into depths yet unspoken." This was clearly not the language or the sentiment of the philosopher-mathematician who had co-authored the *Principia* with Russell. (Russell later confessed that he could not comprehend a word of Whitehead's new philosophy.)

According to Whitehead's new "process" philosophy, most of the models and metaphors employed by philosophers throughout most of the Western tradition have been static metaphors of eternity and timelessness. These metaphors were only reinforced by an interest in the logical foundations of mathematics and the more general fascination with the timeless truths that had captivated the earliest Greek philosophers. Western philosophy is based on such categories as "substance," "essence," and "objects." Its ideals are permanence and logical necessity. There is an alternative metaphor, however, a countercurrent that courses through the history of Western philosophy. It is the metaphor of change, of progress, of process. One finds it in Heraclitus. One finds it even in Aristotle. One finds it in Hegel, Darwin, and Nietzsche.

The most influential figure in the development of this process view of reality was the French philosopher *Henri Bergson* (1859–1941). Bergson's philosophy turned on the idea of *duration*, the reality of change. His point was not just that the properties of things change (blue things turn red, young things turn old), but rather that the stuff of life itself is change. Concepts, he argued, are static and one-sided. When we try to analyze anything, we distort and deform it; we get one view but not another; we freeze the thing in time and fail to understand its development, its *life*. Analysis is, of necessity, always dissatisfied, for there are infinite angles, endless moments.

Bergson was, if indirectly, a different kind of adversary of Russell's logical atomism and his method of analysis. But unlike Russell's other adversaries, Bergson did not just modify the method of analysis. He insisted that in philosophy, we should reject analysis altogether. Metaphysics, he told us, is that discipline which "dispenses with symbols." The metaphysician is thus in the awkward position of having to express the inexpressible. Moreover, Bergson rejected not only the idea of simple facts, simple things, simple sensations, but the very idea of facts, things, and sensations in philosophy. His basic ontology is an ontology of change, not the change of this thing or that property but change as such, change as the whole.

Whitehead, unlike Bergson, retained his love of mathematics, his Platonism regarding "eternal objects," and his keen interest in science, particularly the new physics. But their attack on traditional philosophy is very much the same. The categories of philosophy, Whitehead complained, are left over from seventeenth-century science. They focus on inactive material objects, conceptualize static, "durationless" moments, and distort our experience. They are "indifferent to time." Like Bergson, Whitehead insisted that philosophy adopt a new set of categories. Instead of focusing on objects, it should focus on *events*, conceived of not as static instants (like a "snapshot") but rather as moments in a process of realization. Instead of inanimate objects, Whitehead concentrates on the notion of an organism, "an event, coming into being through patterns." An organism is "vibrant," not static. Whitehead introduced an old Romantic category into twentieth-century philosophy: *creativity*. It is not just that the philosopher should be creative, "speculative," imaginative. Nature itself is continuously creative, novel, imaginative. Accordingly, the task of a philosopher is to invent a poetic language capable of capturing reality as process.

The Tragic Sense of Life: Unamuno, Croce, and Heidegger

Philosophy between the wars was defined by a new pessimism. The horrors of the First World War had killed what was left of the Enlightenment in Europe. Governments were in turmoil, especially in the vanquished countries, Italy and Germany, but also in Spain, which had entered into one of the most brutal civil wars of our time. *Miguel de Unamuno* (1864–1936) was Spain's greatest philosopher, and he took great pride in the fact that his philosophy was distinctively Spanish. He wrote elegantly about the "tragic sense of life," about life filled with anxiety, brutality, and disappointment. He was one of those very individual voices, crying out passionately on the behalf of honesty and integrity, that remind philosophers of their Socratic heritage, of the philosopher as "gadfly" and an expression of what is best in human thought.

Benedetto Croce (1866–1952) was the greatest Italian philosopher since Vico. When Mussolini came to power, Croce was a courageous and outspoken anti-Fascist. His philosophy was political, but it manifested itself as a philosophy of Spirit. His philosophical mentor was Hegel. Croce's philosophy, like Hegel's, emphasized the development of human consciousness, much as his countryman Vico's had also done. But history is undetermined, he insisted. It exhibits spontaneity, unpredictability. It is the work of freedom and of free individuals, who create structures in history rather than discover them. Like Hegel, Croce ultimately concluded that the history of humanity is the emergence of liberty.

Martin Heidegger (1889–1971) was a student of Husserl. But unlike his teacher, he was not primarily concerned with philosophical method or with Husserl's rather bloodless inquiries concerning mathematics and the "formal sciences." Heidegger was a theology student before he became a phenomenologist, and his questions were existential questions, questions about how to live and how to live "authentically," that is, with integrity, in a complex and confusing world. To this end, Heidegger offered a series of provocative but often obscure suggestions, beginning with *Being and Time* (1927).

Turning back to the work of the earliest Greek philosophers, before philosophy became contaminated by metaphysics and subjectivity, Heidegger tried to show us the way to a genuinely holistic philosophy. He rejected the dualism of mind and body, the distinction between subject and object, and the very notions of "consciousness," "experience," and "mind." *Dasein* (literally, "being-there") is the name of the being from whose perspective the world is described. Dasein is "Being-in-the-World," a "unitary phenomenon." Heidegger's early philosophy was largely a search for authenticity, or what might better be described as "own-ness" (*eigentlichkeit*), which would carry us back to the perennial questions about the nature of the self and the meaning of life.

What is the self? It is, at first, merely the roles that other people cast for one, as son, daughter, student, sullen playmate, clever friend. That self, the *das Man* self, is a social construction. There is nothing authentic, nothing that is *my own*, about it. The authentic self, by contrast, is discovered in profound moments of unique self-recognition, notably, when one faces one's own "Being-unto-Death." It is not enough to acknowledge that "we are all going to die." That, according to Heidegger, is merely an objective truth and still inauthentic. It is *one's own* death that matters here, and one's "own-ness" thus becomes facing up to one's own mortality. We saw a similar thesis in Unamuno, and in this sense, at least, Heidegger too acknowledges the "tragic sense of life."

Heidegger's philosophy was a monumental achievement, one of the most powerful and influential philosophies of the century. But as an example, Heidegger does not pass with flying colors. Whereas both Unamuno and Croce denounced the Fascists and risked the consequences, Heidegger joined the Nazi Party in 1933. (He quit the following year.) His infamous flirtation with the Nazis raises the difficult question "Did his philosophy express his politics, his character?"

Reactions to Fascism: Positivism and Existentialism

The Second World War began in 1939, and so did the Nazis' attempted extermination of European Jews, along with Catholics, gypsies, homosexuals, and other minorities. The rise of the Nazis, the rumbles of war, and the horrors of the concentration camp stimulated two radical philosophical movements, one of them frontally attacking irrationality in all of its forms and the other acknowledging irrationality as the human condition but confronting it with responsibility. The first, known as *logical positivism*, was loosely based on the early philosophy of Wittgenstein and traced itself back to Hume and the British empiricists. It prided itself on being hardheaded and scientific and tolerating no nonsense. The other, called *existentialism*, was drawn from Kierkegaard and Nietzsche, using Husserl's phenomenology as its method. Whatever their considerable differences, both movements endorsed unsentimental honesty.

The logical positivists, insisting on scientific and logical rigor and blaming the careless grandiosity of German romanticism for the horrors of National Socialism, pushed questions of value to the side. Like Wittgenstein at the end of the *Tractatus*, they seemed to insist that nothing intelligible could be said about such matters. Bertrand Russell had argued that ethics is simply subjective, a matter of emotion rather than logic and rationality, and the positivists agreed. But that left the status of ethics dubious or, at best, dangling. If philosophers were not in a position to chastise the sins of the world, then who would be? The logical positivists fought to keep the Enlightenment alive, but they brought about the virtual exile of ethics from philosophy.

Many of the early positivists were physicists and mathematicians as well as philosophers. Their bias was heavily toward the sciences, and their method began with a sharp distinction between facts and values. The positivists' primary concern was to separate the meaningful hypotheses that science could and should consider from those that were meaningless, a waste of time, and only a source of unresolvable disagreement. They found their standard, their cutting instrument, in the notion of *verifiability*. A hypothesis—and this was quickly expanded to include any sentence whatever—was meaningful only insofar as it could be verified by the evidence. There is more than enough nonsense in the world, claimed the positivists, and it is the job of philosophers, to the best of their abilities, to make sure that there is no more of it.

Oddly enough, the existentialists, perhaps the most moralistic or, in any case, moralizing philosophers of the twentieth century, also seemed to avoid ethics. Heidegger emphatically insisted that he was not offering any ethics, and he continued to speak with disdain about those who "fish in the false sea of values." His own political choices seemed to confirm the amorality of his ideas. Even *Jean-Paul Sartre* (1905–1980), moralist *par excellence*, followed Heidegger in insisting that his existentialism was not as such an ethical philosophy. But what the existentialists were rejecting was a certain thin, "bourgeois" conception of morality, the kind of ethics that worries about keeping your promises, paying your debts, and avoiding scandal. The watchword of the existentialists' philosophy, "authenticity," was a call to integrity, a call for responsibility, even, in wartime, a call to heroism.

EXISTENTIALISM WAS A philosophical movement that included Kierkegaard, perhaps Nietzsche, Unamuno, and Heidegger. One might add Fyodor Dostoyevsky and the Czech writer Franz Kafka. It should certainly include the French-Algerian writer *Albert Camus*

(1913–1960). Some enthusiasts have traced the movement all the way back to Socrates, but the term "existentialism" was coined by Sartre. Kierkegaard's work inspired an influential school of twentieth-century religious existentialists (including Paul Tillich, Martin Buber, Karl Barth, and Gabriel Marcel), but many of the existentialists were atheists, notably Nietzsche, Sartre, and Camus, who called religious belief a form of "philosophical suicide."

One would not go wrong in saying that existentialism represented an attitude particularly appropriate for modern (even "postmodern") mass society. If we may generalize for just a moment, we might suggest that the existentialists shared a concern for the individual and personal responsibility. They tended to be suspicious of or hostile to the submersion of the individual in larger public groups or forces. Thus Kierkegaard and Nietzsche both attacked "the herd," and Heidegger distinguished "authentic existence" from mere social ("*das Man*") existence. Sartre, in particular, emphasized the importance of free individual choice in the face of the power of other people to influence and coerce our desires, beliefs, and decisions. Here he followed Kierkegaard especially, for whom passionate, personal choice and commitment are essential for true "existence."

Retreating from Heidegger's attack on the Cartesian view of consciousness, Sartre argued that consciousness (described as "being-for-itself") is such that it is always free to choose (though not free not to choose) and free to "negate" (or reject) the given features of the world. One may be born Jewish or black, French or crippled, but it is an open question what one will make of oneself, whether these unchosen facts will be made into handicaps or advantages, challenges to be negotiated or excuses to do nothing. One may be cowardly or shy, but such behavior is always a choice, and one can always resolve to change. Sartre's stern philosophy would have a particular poignance in the midst of the horrors of war and the Nazi occupation of France.

Camus was a novelist and essayist rather than a formal philosopher, but he captured the "sensibility" of the century with his dramatic notion of "the Absurd." The Absurd is a metaphysical sense of confrontation between our demands for rationality and justice, on the one hand, and an "indifferent universe," on the other. In *The Myth of Sisyphus*, Camus compared the ancient Greek figure of Sisyphus, who was condemned to spend all of eternity pushing a rock up a mountain, to the fate of all of us. We expend all of our energy pushing our weight against futility and frustration. Camus presented the primary question of philosophy, accordingly, as the question of whether life is worth living, or, differently put, whether we ought to commit suicide. His answer to the first is an enthusiastic "yes," to the second, a moralistic "no." Camus's Sisyphus, instructively, threw himself into his meaningless project and thereby made it meaningful. "One must consider Sisyphus happy," concluded Camus, and so, too, might we be if we acknowledged and threw ourselves into our own lives and, Camus adds, if we help others.

Gabriel Marcel (1889–1973) similarly portrayed what he called "a broken world," a world of emptiness in which philosophy had been reduced to mere "problems" and the mysteries of human life systematically denied or ignored. But Marcel, unlike Camus, was a man of God, and like Kierkegaard, he insisted that we face up to the most profound experiences in life without the false front of objectivity, that is, without putting those experiences at a distance as mere problems to be solved. There is no "solution" to life, love, or death. These are the mysteries that provide meaning to human life.

One of the persistent errors in the understanding of existentialism is to confuse its emphasis on "meaning" and "meaninglessness" with an advocacy of despair or existential *angst*. Even Camus insisted that the Absurd is not license for despair, and Nietzsche encouraged our "cheerfulness." Kierkegaard wrote of "glad tidings," and for both Heidegger and Sartre the much celebrated emotion of *angst* was essential to the human condition as a symptom of freedom and self-awareness, not as a reason to despair.

Simone de Beauvoir (1908–1986) was a philosopher and novelist who shared with Sartre this emphasis on freedom and on responsibility for what one is and "what one makes of what is made of one." She spelled out, as he had not, the ethical implications of Sartre's existentialism. Beauvoir was always fascinated by her society's oblivion or resistance to sensitive topics, and she was appalled that her society, and virtually all societies, gave very little attention to the problems and inequities afflicting the female half of humanity. Accordingly, she applied her existentialist theories to the special "existential" circumstances of being a woman in *The Second Sex* (1949), ultimately one of the most influential books of the century.

Philosophy Discovers "the Other": The Question of Postmodernism

Simone de Beauvoir sparked an important question: Where are all the women? Western philosophy has historically discussed or included women only as an afterthought, if at all. Some feminists have suggested that philosophy has been based on a "masculine" style of disputation and confrontation exemplified by Socrates. But whatever else it may have been, philosophy has always been a refuge, a luxury enjoyed primarily by those who have (one way or another) been free from the demands of exhausting physical labor, earning a living, or cleaning and caring for a household. For that reason, it should not be surprising that most of the men we have discussed, and many of the greatest philosophers, were gentlemen bachelors (or, often, priests). Surprisingly few talk very much about the family, and interpersonal relationships in general play an embarrassingly minuscule role in the history of Western philosophy.

Then, again, making a name for yourself in philosophy depends not just on talent but on time, teachers, colleagues, an audience, publishers, readers, and one's students. The sad truth is that women have been shut out at virtually every level of philosophical success. Relatively few women have been allowed even to become interested in philosophy. Before this century, few women were admitted to the appropriate schools, and those who were allowed to study philosophy (some of the students of Plato and Pythagoras, for example) were rarely allowed to achieve stature. If a woman did manage to disseminate some ideas of her own and attract a following, she would rarely be recognized as "one of the boys," in all probability remaining unpublished and unknown. If she was published, her books did not survive. The absence of women in philosophy was not, we can be sure, due to lack of talent. But no woman philosopher ever found her Plato, as did Socrates, to carry her legend to posterity. (If there was such a Plato, she evidently never got published, either.).

Feminist philosophy challenges the entire Western tradition (and not only that tradition). While claiming to be universal and all-inclusive, philosophy has not even included or taken account of the woman next door. It certainly has not asked whether she sees things differently, or whether she would ask the same questions in the same way as male philosophers. Thus one of the most radical changes that feminism has provoked in contemporary philosophy is the centrality of the notion of a personal "standpoint"—what Nietzsche called a "perspective." Different people, in different positions, might "see" the world very differently. Thus, a plurality of perspectives might replace the competing demands for a singular "objectivity."

THE SAME CHARGE extends to the neglect of the rest of the world. Only recently have American and European philosophers generally started to take seriously the ancient philosophical traditions of Asia, and only more recently has there been even a glimmer of interest in the "Third World," despite an unprecedented degree of interaction, intermingling, and confrontation between cultural groups. As the world gets smaller, there are growing concerns about the way cultural groups can and should live together. Philosophy should become a major intermediary in this process.

The most successful philosophy for this purpose, at least until very recently, has been Marxism. Soon after the Second World War, Mao Zedong overthrew the traditional government of China with a "peasant revolt" that pricked up the ears of every oppressed people in the world. Marxism was aggressively synthesized with local traditions and concepts. One might argue that Marxism appropriated Confucianism, with its emphasis on supreme personal and family authority, now focussing on Mao the patriach. Like most revolutionary governments, Mao's new China took on many of the worst oppressive habits of its predecessors, but the Maoist revolution continues to beckon to poor and oppressed peoples across the world. An equally stunning contrast to Mao's violent revolution, however, was Mahatma Gandhi's "nonviolent resistance" against the British in India. As Asia gains in prominence and economic power in the modern world, and as Africa and the other Americas emerge to claim their heritage, modern philosophy cannot but be affected by this twin set of dramatic examples, a philosophy of revolution and the philosophy of nonviolence.

Philosophy, in the West, has until recently been treated as a uniquely Western tradition. We want to insist, to the contrary, that philosophy has appeared almost everywhere. There is no single philosophical perspective, no one "correct" philosophical method, no unique and "true" philosophy. The movement in modern philosophy that begins with the New Science and Descartes is but one set of claims among many.

Not surprisingly, this rejection of traditional "modern" philosophy has itself become a philosophy. *Postmodernism* is a rag-tag "movement" that insists that overly authoritarian, unapologetically Western philosophy has run its course. Feminism and multiculturalism, postmodernists argue, are two powerful pieces of evidence that this is so. Philosophy, the search for a single truth, no longer exists. There are only philosophies. Indeed, there is no longer Truth, only "discourses"—people talking, thinking, writing, broadcasting. There is no longer a center, a "mainstream" in philosophy, only rapidly expanding margins and numerous streams and puddles. Postmodernism, if its advocates are to be believed, signals the end of the Western philosophical tradition.

Nevertheless, we might, in closing, consider the phenomenon sometimes labeled *New Age* philosophy, an amazing collection of ideas from healthy whole-earth thinking to loony-tunes from the edge. But the evident hunger for philosophy that "New Age" phenomena reveal does suggest an important prognosis for philosophy, despite the doomsday warnings from the postmodernists and the desiccation that has come to define so much of academic philosophy. What remains is a need for philosophy complicated by a new global awareness. As philosophers, we cannot help being excited by the bewildering variety of ideas, the dynamism of ongoing confrontations. But at the same time, we are disturbed by the fact that the old ideal of philosophy, as a search for wisdom rather than a peculiar professional skill or a merely clever game, has gotten lost.

Philosophy has always been representative of what is most human about us. Perhaps what we need is not more sophistication but more openness. We need to be not more clever but, rather, better listeners. What philosophy is, after all, is a thoughtful openness to the world, a passion for wisdom.

A Brief Bibliography

We have not included classic texts, which are widely available in various editions. We recommend the books listed here for those who want further reading on the history of philosophy.

General Introductions

Copelston, Frederick. *The History of Philosophy*. 9 vols. Rev. ed. Westminster, Maryland: The Newman Press, 1946–1974.

Durant, Will and Ariel. *The Story of Philosophy*. 9 vols. New York: Simon and Schuster, 1935f.

Flew, Anthony, *An Introduction to Western Philosophy*. London: Thames & Hudson, 1971.

Jones, W. T. *A History of Western Philosophy*. 4 vols. New York: Harcourt, Brace & World, 1969.

Parkinson, G. H. R., and S. G. Shanker, eds. *The Routledge History of Philosophy*. 10 vols. London: Routledge, 1993f.

Russell, Bertrand. *History of Western Philosophy*. New York: Simon and Schuster, 1945.

Smart, Ninian. *The Long Search*. Boston: Little, Brown, and Company, 1977.

Smith, Huston. *The Religions of Man*. New York: Harper & Row, 1958.

Solomon, Robert C. *Introducing Philosophy*. 6th ed. Fort Worth: Harcourt, Brace, 1997.

Solomon, Robert C., and Kathleen M. Higgins. *A Short History of Philosophy*. Oxford: Oxford University Press, 1996.

Solomon, Robert C., and Kathleen M. Higgins. *From Africa to Zen: An Invitation to World Philosophy*. Lanham, Md.: Rowman and Littlefield, 1992.

Tarnas, Richard. *The Passion of the Western Mind*. New York: Harmony, 1991.

Whitehead, Alfred North. *Adventures of Ideas*. New York: Macmillan, 1933.

Books on Specific Topics

Abraham, W. E. *The Mind of Africa*. Chicago: University of Chicago Press, 1962.

Allinson, Robert E., ed. *Understanding the Chinese Mind*. Hong Kong: Oxford University Press, 1989.

Ames, Roger T., and David L. Hall. *Thinking Through Confucius*. Albany, N.Y.: State University of New York Press, 1987.

Appiah, Kwame Anthony. *In My Father's House: Africa in the Philosophy of Culture*. New York: Oxford University Press, 1992.

Barnes, Hazel. *Sartre*. Philadelphia: Lippincott, 1973.

Barnes, Jonathan. *Aristotle*. New York: Oxford University Press, 1982.

Beck, Lewis White, ed. *Eighteenth-Century Philosophy*. New York: The Free Press, 1966.

Benedict, Ruth. *The Chrysanthemum and the Sword: Patterns of Japanese Culture*. Boston: Houghton Mifflin, 1946.

Brown, Joseph E. *The Spiritual Legacy of the American Indian*. New York: Crossroad, 1984.

Burnet, J. *Early Greek Philosophy*. 4th ed. London: Black, 1930.

Cassier, Ernst. *The Individual and the Cosmos in Renaissance Philosophy*. Trans. Mario Domandi. New York: Barnes and Noble, 1963.

Chadwick, Henry. *History and Thought of the Early Church*. London: Variorum Reprints, 1982.

Clendinnen, Inga. *Aztecs*. Cambridge: Cambridge University Press, 1991.

Cornford, Francis M. *Before and After Socrates*. Cambridge: Cambridge University Press, 1932.

Crawford, William Rex. *A Century of Latin American Thought*. Cambridge, Mass.: Harvard University Press, 1944.

Crow Dog, Mary. *Lakota Woman*. New York: HarperCollins, 1990.

Dodds, Eric Robertson. *The Greeks and the Irrational*. Berkeley: University of California Press, 1951.

Farrington, Benjamin. *Greek Science*. New York: Penguin, 1944.

Fogelin, Robert. *Wittgenstein*. London: Routledge, 1983.

Fung, Yu-Lan. *A Short History of Chinese Philosophy*. Edited by Derk Bodde. New York: Macmillan, 1948.

Glanville, Stephen. *The Legacy of Egypt*. Oxford: Clarendon, 1947.

Guignon, Charles, ed. *The Cambridge Companion to Heidegger*. Cambridge: Cambridge University Press, 1993.

Guthrie, W. K. C. *Greek Philosophy*. London: Methuen, 1950.

Gyekye, Kwame. *An Essay on African Philosophical Thought*. New York: Cambridge University Press, 1987.

Hourani, Albert. *A History of the Arab Peoples*. Cambridge, Mass.: Harvard University Press, 1991.

Jacobson, Dan. *The Story of the Stories: The Chosen People and Its God*. New York: Harper and Row, 1982.

Janik, A., and S. Toulmin. *Wittgenstein's Vienna*. New York: Simon and Schuster, 1993.

Katz, Steven T. *Jewish Philosophers*. New York: Bloch, 1975.

Kenny, Anthony. Descartes: A Study of His Philosophy. New York: Random House, 1968.

Kirk, G. S., and Raven, J.E. *The Pre-Socratic Philosophers*. Cambridge: Cambridge University Press, 1957.

Knowles, David. *The Evolution of Medieval Thought*. London: Longman, 1962.

Lloyd, Genevieve. *The Man of Reason: "Male and "Female" in Western Philosophy*. Minneapolis: University of Minnesota Press, 1984.

Mackey, Louis. *Kierkegaard: A Kind of Poet*. Philadelphia: University of Pennsylvania Press, 1971.

Magnus, Bernd., and Kathleen M. Higgins, K. *The Cambridge Companion to Nietzsche*. Cambridge: Cambridge University Press, 1996.

Malandra, William W., trans. and ed. *An Introduction to Ancient Iranian Religion*. Minneapolis: University of Minnesota Press, 1983.

McVeigh, Malcolm. *God in Africa: Conceptions of God in African Traditional Religion and Christianity*. Cape Cod, Mass.: C. Stark, 1974.

Miller, James. *Rousseau and Democracy*. New Haven: Yale University Press, 1984.

Myers, Gerald. *William James*. New Haven: Yale University Press, 1986.

Nicholson, Linda J., ed. *Feminism/Postmodernism*. New York: Routledge, 1990.

O'Flaherty, Wendy Doniger, ed. and trans. *Hindu Myths: A Sourcebook Translated from the Sanskrit*. Baltimore: Penguin, 1975.

Overholt, Thomas W., and J. Baird Calicott. *Clothed-in-Fur and Other Tales: An Introduction to an Ojibwa World View*. Washington, D.C.: University Press of America, 1982.

Phillips, Anthony. *God, B.C.* Oxford: Oxford University Press, 1977.

Phillips, Stephen H. *Aurobindo's Philosophy of Brahman*. Leiden: Brill, 1986.

Schacht, Richard. *Nietzsche*. London: Routledge, 1983.

Skorupski, John. *English-Language Philosophy 1750–1945*. Oxford: Oxford University Press, 1992.

Sluga, Hans. *Heidegger's Crisis*. Cambridge, Mass.: Harvard University Press, 1993.

Solomon, Robert C. *Continental Philosophy since 1750: The Rise and Fall of the Self*. Oxford: Oxford University Press, 1988.

Solomon, Robert C. *From Rationalism to Existentialism: The Existentialists and Their Nineteenth-Century Backgrounds*. New York: Harper & Row, 1972.

Solomon, Robert C. *In the Spirit of Hegel*. New York: Oxford University Press, 1983.

Spiegelberg, H. *The Phenomenological Movement*. The Hague: Nijhoff, 1962.

Stone, Isidor F. *The Trial of Socrates*. Boston: Little, Brown, and Company, 1988.

Tanner, Michael. *Nietzsche*. Oxford: Oxford University Press, 1995.

Taylor, Alfred E. *Aristotle*. Mineola, N.Y.: Dover, 1955.

Taylor, Alfred E. *Socrates*. Garden City, N.Y.: Doubleday, 1953.

Taylor, Mark *Journeys to Selfhood: Hegel and Kierkegaard*. Berkeley: University of California Press, 1980.

Toulmin, Stephen. *Cosmopolis: The Hidden Agenda of Modernity*. New York: Macmillan, 1990.

Underhill, Ruth M. *Red Man's Religion: Beliefs and Practices of the Indians North of Mexico*. Chicago: University of Chicago Press, 1965.

Vignaux, Paul. *Philosophy in the Middle Ages: An Introduction*. Translated by E. C. Hall. New York: Meridian, 1959.

Walsh, Michael. *Roots of Christianity*. London: Grafton, 1986.

Whale, J. S., D. D. *The Protestant Tradition: An Essay in Interpretation*. Cambridge: Cambridge University Press, 1955.

White, M. *The Philosophy of the American Revolution*. New York: Oxford University Press, 1978.

Wing-Tsit Chan, ed. *A Source Book in Chinese Philosophy*. Princeton, N.J.: Princeton University Press, 1963.

Woolhouse, R. S. *The Empiricists*. New York: Oxford University Press, 1988.

Zea, Leopoldo. *The Latin American Mind*. Trans. J. H. Abbot and L. Dunham. Norman, Ok.: University of Oklahoma, 1963.

Index